US
AGAINST
THE WORLD

US
AGAINST
THE WORLD

Our Secrets to Love, Marriage, and Family

DAVID and TAMELA MANN

with Shaun Saunders

W PUBLISHING GROUP

AN IMPRINT OF THOMAS NELSON

Published in Nashville, Tennessee, by W Publishing, an imprint of Thomas Nelson.

Thomas Nelson titles may be purchased in bulk for educational, business, fund-raising, or sales promotional use. For information, please e-mail SpecialMarkets@ ThomasNelson.com.

Unless otherwise noted, Scripture quotations are taken from THE ENGLISH STANDARD VERSION. © 2001 by Crossway Bibles, a division of Good News Publishers.

Scripture quotations marked NIV are taken from the Holy Bible, New International Version®, NIV®. Copyright © 1973, 1978, 1984, 2011 by Biblica, Inc.™ Used by permission of Zondervan. All rights reserved worldwide. www.zondervan.com

"Secret Lovers" lyrics used with permission from David Lewis and Wayne Lewis.

ISBN 978-1-4041-0920-9 (custom)
ISBN 978-0-7852-2009-1 (HC)
ISBN 978-0-7852-2017-6 (eBook)

Library of Congress Cataloging-in-Publication Data

Library of Congress Control Number: 2018952375

Printed in the United States of America

18 19 20 21 22 DP 10 9 8 7 6 5 4 3 2 1

TAMELA:

This book is dedicated to my late mother, "Madea" Mary Elizabeth Sample. You always told me, "Love the Lord with all your heart, and the Lord will take you far." Your prayers, wisdom, knowledge, and nurturing care helped groom me into the woman, wife, mother, grandmother, and servant I am today. There is no way I would be where I am if it hadn't been for your love and guidance. I miss you and wish you were here to celebrate with me all the things you prayed for.

DAVID:

This book is dedicated to my mom, Sandra Etta Mann. Your prayers, sacrifice, love, and guidance have shaped me to become the leader, husband, father, and grandfather I am today. I learned from watching you that hard work truly pays off, and for that I am forever grateful. This book is also dedicated to my late grandfather, Roy "Duke" Mann. You taught me to be a godly man and the value of being a faithful husband and family man. Thank you for the example and for speaking success into me early. I miss you, and I love you.

TOGETHER:

We dedicate this book to our children: Sonya, Porcia, Tiffany, David Jr., and Tia. You all have pushed us to be better parents. Even when we didn't make the right parenting choices, you still loved us without condition. Thank y'all for blessing us with an abundance of grandchildren who keep us on our toes, keep us busy, and keep us young. Thank you for believing in Mama and Daddy. We love y'all.

CONTENTS

CONTENTS

FOREWORD

When I envision marriage, I think about my mother and father, who were together for more than forty years. Despite the longevity of their marriage, my mother received no love, no support, no encouragement—nothing positive. So, from childhood on, I've looked at marriage as a pretty miserable institution, a losing proposition. And truthfully, I've become more than a little cynical about the whole thing.

For instance, it's not unusual for me to come to work and find someone huddled at their desk in tears. "What's going on?" I'll ask. And nine times out of ten, they'll tell me it's their marriage. They're going through a separation or a divorce.

How strange, I think to myself. Two people love each other so dearly and passionately that they have a wedding, get married, and receive a piece of paper that legally binds them together. Yet that very piece of paper can ultimately end up tearing them apart.

I've seen marriages end tragically. I've seen them lead to bankruptcy. I've seen children used as pawns. I've seen the worst come up in souls.

Yet, despite my cynicism around marriage, for some reason, people still come to me for counseling about their relationships. I know in my heart that I'm not the one to ask. So I flip through my Rolodex, looking for people with great marriages, those who can offer good advice. I'll tell you, it's not a long list; I can probably name them on one hand. But at the top of my list, a couple who always shines the brightest is David and Tamela Mann.

Up close, I've witnessed how much these two people support, love, and care for each other. I've seen David's heart open when he looks at Tamela. And I've seen the way Tam always steps up to unconditionally support David. I've watched the way they both love their children without end.

That said, I know their marriage hasn't been easy. They've had to endure a lot of trials. Through it all, they put God first. They hold a powerful, abiding faith. And that's why their marriage is profoundly beautiful, strong, solid, and innocent. It exemplifies the fruits of the Spirit.

When I think about David and Tam and the love they share, all the horrible things I've heard about marriage, all the terrible things I've seen, and all the horrors I grew up watching are chipped away—and in their place, slivers of light and hope shine through.

For these reasons, I'm honored to be writing this foreword. The Manns' relationship is the way a marriage should be: ordained before God. It's the model. It's the ideal. Their type of love, guided by honor and respect, is what can heal couples.

David and Tamela are here to offer their love and wisdom in *Us Against the World*. Their experience, understanding, faith, and love are invaluable. Take heart.

—Tyler Perry

INTRODUCTION

Can we just be honest a minute? Marriage is hard work. Two independent lives are merging. Two different mind-sets are colliding. Two different people are learning. Two different households are shifting. Two different philosophies on money, sex, parenting, love, and communication are blending. This is no easy feat. This is, sometimes, a big hot mess. But for us, marriage has been life's greatest gift.

It's amazing what's possible when two people are willing to do the work. Joy-filled marriages don't happen because we wish for them. They don't happen because we buy a pretty ring and slip it on a beautiful lady's finger. They happen when friendship is the foundation, when faith is your bedrock, and when fun is an absolute nonnegotiable.

In the Mann household, I told Tamela long ago that it's us against the world. She agreed! And we have been laughing and loving and singing together ever since.

MEET THE MANNS

Our life as David and Tamela Mann began many years ago in Fort Worth, Texas. From high school besties to eternal lovers, we have seen the hand of God keep us and keep our family. Our beginnings are humble. Our experiences are quite normal—for the most part. We have been blessed to see the world through the lens of many amazing opportunities, but our family is just like your family. Our marriage is just like your marriage. If you've argued about it, so have we. But we determined to never let a bad day turn into a bad life.

Tam and I both grew up with wonderful mothers, absent fathers, and dysfunctional patterns. Our families were poor, but they loved us so well that we thought we were rich. When we met as teenagers, we discovered a mutual passion for God, music, and family. We became best friends. We decided to build a life together. We had a three-dimensional goal when we got married: to love God, to love each other, and to inspire our children to see marriage differently.

MEET OUR KIDS ·

Our dream was to get married, have children, and live happily ever after. But life doesn't always give us what we dream. It gives us what we can handle. So God allowed several things to happen the way he wanted them to happen. As a result, our family is not just blended. We are super-blended! Sonya is our oldest daughter. She joined our family at fourteen when her mother passed away. We were twenty-two, and she was a teenager—not much younger than we were, really. Sonya witnessed her mom get shot in the head. Then she nursed her mom through the heart-wrenching difficulty of terminal cancer and saw her mom breathe her last breath. Sonya is our resilient survivor. She became a reliable pillar for us when we first got married. She taught us how to turn lemons into lemonade.

Porcia is our next-oldest daughter. Born in 1986, Porcia came out of the womb making peace. She was the peacemaker between her mom and dad, and she continues to be the mediator of conflict in our family today. Whenever disputes break out, we can count on Porcia to help us find resolution. Even as a child, she helped her brother and sisters figure out how to work through their issues. Her gift is that she listens well, and she doesn't take sides.

Tiffany came next, in 1987, and she was the greatest surprise our family has ever received. For as long as Tiffany has been alive, she has been a grinder. Tiffany can do anything she puts her mind to—whether it is singing, acting, or dancing—you name it, she's done it. Her ability to thrive in any environment is her superpower. She's also funny and sarcastic. (One can only guess where she picked up those traits.)

Then there was David Jr. David was unique from conception. He is the only boy born to us, and the child who tries to give us a heart attack once a year. David is the fire starter in our family. If trouble is happening in our home, you can bet David Jr. is somewhere close to it. David has always been our carefree, passionate, and brilliant child. His gift is his determination. David Jr. is our utility man. If a job needs to get done, we know he will make it happen. He is reliable. He is loyal. He is dependable.

Finally, we have Tia. She is the baby of our family, and as the baby, she is a baby! The kids always say that Tia is Tamela's favorite child, but Tam will neither deny nor confirm these allegations. Tia is not the hardest worker in our family, but she is the greatest giver of our family. No child can compete with Tia's heart. She will give her last dime to help those she loves. She is a caring soul, a nurturer, and a spoiled brat! But we love her, and we love our entire family.

THE HEART OF OUR FAMILY

Throughout the years of singing, performing, acting, movies, plays, albums, and tours, our family has kept Tamela and me together. But it's our marriage that's at the center of it all. Some have called us slightly dysfunctional because Tam and I can only go a few hours before we must be around each other again, but that's okay—we put the *fun* in dysfunctional. We've learned how to work together as partners, play together as lovers, learn together as students, and build together as dreamers. We have not had a perfect marriage or a perfect family, but we believe we have a few secrets that can help you to strengthen your marriage.

In this book, you will learn about a few of our secrets to love, marriage, and family. Over these last thirty years, our love has shaped us, our marriage has secured us, and our family has supported us. In the first section, we begin with our love story. We tell you everything—how we met, how we fell in love, how our picture-perfect life shifted unexpectedly, and how our relationship endured the test of time. As you read, you will learn who we are—the good, the bad, and the ugly. You will discover details about our lives that have shaped us for the better. The drama, the pain, the passion, and the joy—all of it taught us something unique about life that has forever impacted our perspective on love and marriage. We share these stories to encourage you to find the blessing in your story too.

> **We've learned how to work together as partners, play together as lovers, learn together as students, and build together as dreamers.**

We've also tried to share some things along the way that have helped us to build and sustain our marriage. We believe marriages thrive because of commitment, communication, celebration, compassion, collaboration, and cooperation. We believe that marriages can shift from average to amazing when forgiveness, laughter, intimacy, and faith are at the center of your relationship. We believe in the power of marriage. We believe in marital partnership. Not only is marriage a God-ordained relationship, but it is an amazing journey to explore with your ride-or-die friend. In addition to helping you discover more about who we are as a married couple, in part 2 we share prayers and discussion questions at the end of each chapter. And there are even a few activities for you to consider incorporating into your marriage. These tools have been a tremendous blessing to us, and we hope they'll help you to strengthen your marriage, so that in the end you can also say, "It's *us* against the world!"

Ultimately, our desire is to inspire you to believe in marriage like we do. We know what the statistics suggest. We are aware of the many things that break marriages apart. But if, by the end of this book, we've encouraged you to try again, believe again, hope again, and give marriage your best shot, then we have accomplished our purpose.

PART 1

HOW WE GOT HERE

CHAPTER 1

HUMBLE BEGINNINGS

Before We Were Mann and Wife for Life

My favorite childhood memory is not paying bills.
—BILL MURRAY

Chances are, if you know me, David Mann, then you know my wife, Tamela Mann. We are a package deal. Years ago, this beautiful woman and I fell in love and made a commitment. We committed to love together, live together, dream together, create together, and play together. And, together, we never looked back! Sure, we have different talents and gifts. Tamela, obviously, is an incredibly anointed singer with a flair for fashion and a heart of gold. I'm the funny one. And sure, sometimes the world says, "Good job, Tamela! Here's your Grammy!" or, "All right, David! Here's an Image Award for you!" Those accolades we get as individuals are valuable to us only when we are sharing the joys—and the sorrows—together. We are first and always a team. I cannot imagine my life without her. When

Tam and I talk about where we are today and how much we have been blessed, we see how it all started long before we ever met. Right, Momma?

That's right, David. Tell them how it all started.

DAVID ON THE MOVE FROM THE GET-GO

The beginning of life shapes you for the rest of your life. I might not have enjoyed every moment of my childhood, but I wouldn't change a bit of my journey now. If every twist and turn happened so I could be where I am today, then every tear and every year was worth it.

I was born in Lubbock, Texas, to an incredibly resilient woman. My mother, Sandra Mann, was not only the rock of our family but also a miracle worker. Somehow, with just a seventh grade education and living on a very limited income, she raised five strong sons by herself. And she taught us to be honorable, honest, and holy.

I am the second oldest of five. Each of us had a different father. From my mother, I learned who to be. From my father, I learned who *not* to be. In more than fifty years of living, I saw my father about six times. I had one conversation with him a few years ago. Six months after that, my father died.

Mom had her first child at fourteen. She had me at sixteen. She was a baby having babies, and she experienced a lot of difficulty because of it. My grandparents forced her to quit school in the seventh grade. Because she was so young, the family judged her harshly. The community she grew up in labeled her "damaged goods." It's a shame, really. Mom had so many natural talents and skills that she could've become whatever she put her mind to, but she had no one to help her. No one was willing to mold her, nurture her, or see her—really *see* her. So, like many people who have been overlooked and rejected, Mom searched for love in all the wrong places.

What I remember most about growing up is that we were always moving. Not long after my second or third birthday, we moved from Lubbock, Texas. My mother got married for the first time, and we moved to St. Louis. But that was only a pit stop. Before we could get accustomed to our new home, the relationship between my mother and her first husband became more than toxic—it was outright abusive. So my mom packed me and my little brother up and left with only what she could carry in her hands. We boarded a train in the middle of the day while her husband was at work and headed back to Lubbock, Texas. A year or so later, my mother met a nice young man who ended up becoming her boyfriend. Then came another move—this time to California. The weather there was sunny and hot, but their relationship was cloudy and cold. Within a year's time, child number four was added to the bunch, and we found ourselves circling back to Fort Worth, where marriage number two was now in the mix. After my last brother was born, we moved back to Lubbock, and from Lubbock we moved to Houston. (Too bad I didn't get frequent flyer miles for all of that moving.) When Houston didn't work out, we moved back to Fort Worth—the city where I graduated from the one and only Oscar Dean Wyatt High School. That's where I met a beautiful, light-skinned girl named Tamela Johnson.

TAM'S TURN

I was born Tamela Jean Johnson, the youngest of fourteen kids. I stuck out like a sore thumb. I was lighter than any of my siblings, so they called me the "white sheep" of the family. I was the baby too. Most of my brothers and sisters were grown by the time I was born, so I had to figure out a lot of things on my own. Couple that with the fact that I had a different father from the rest of my brothers and sisters. Plus, I was the only one in my family to graduate from high school. So trust me: my family didn't know what to do with me. But eventually they figured it out.

I grew up in Fort Worth, Texas. We moved some, but my family didn't move around as much as David's. My mother tried to keep us together as much as possible, but with fourteen children, it wasn't the easiest thing to do. Momma was a praying woman. She was a faithful woman. She took her walk with God seriously. She knew she couldn't give us much, but she gave us God—and that was more than enough for me. Of the many gifts she gave me as a child, the greatest gift was my relationship with Christ.

I guess you could say I grew up in a single-parent home. I had a couple of stepfathers over the years, and our family was very blended, but my mother was the permanent fixture in my life. My biological father wasn't around, and sometimes my stepfathers were there, sometimes they weren't. The closest thing I had to a father figure was my mother's second husband, Mr. Doll Cooper. Mr. Cooper loved my mother and always wanted her to reach for the stars. He tried to help her rise beyond her third-grade level of education, and I believe he wanted to get Mom out of poverty. But she never did. It's so ironic because my mother had so much faith in God and could believe God for everybody else, but I don't think she had enough faith to come out of poverty. Mr. Doll was sent by God to help her see life differently.

When I was twelve years old, Mr. Doll Cooper died. He had plenty of land, houses, cars, and property, but when his family came to the funeral, they claimed all of his possessions and left my mother with nothing. She had helped him to build and sustain his life, and they left her with nothing. She was there when he took his last breath, and even though they had their ups and downs, his family didn't think enough about her or her fourteen kids to leave her a car to ride in. Mr. Doll was my mother's everything, so when he passed away, she had nothing to build from. Man, he was a gift. He wasn't perfect but he was a good guy. I always felt like if Mr. Doll had lived, not only would he have helped my mother to change her mind-set, but he would've also helped me to take my education more seriously. I believe I eventually would've gone to college.

But we were poor. Who was going to pay for college? My brothers had social security checks coming in, and my mother received a welfare check every month. That's how we survived. My family made it on two fish, five loaves, and a lot of faith. I guess that's why ownership is so important to me now. My mother never owned anything, and I believe that affected her. She didn't own a car. She didn't own a house. She rented houses and borrowed cars, but she never had property in her name. My uncles and aunts did, but my mother didn't have anything to call her own. As a result, she settled for what people told her she could have instead of dreaming big enough to get what she deserved.

SALVATION SONG

When I turned eight, I accepted Jesus Christ as Lord and Savior of my life. Though I was young, I was serious about my journey. I'll never forget my first choir solo, "I Don't Feel No Ways Tired," by James Cleveland. I sang it all the time, and when I got to the bridge, "I don't believe He's brought me this far to leave me," tears just rolled down my face. I wept and wept as I sang. My ad-libs reminded the congregation that God had kept my momma, and God had kept my family, and before I knew it, the church was standing and praising God with me!

Now, remember, I was eight. I hadn't been through a whole lot, but I had seen enough to know that God was faithful. Faith is funny like that sometimes. Some might think, *How can an eight-year-old girl be able to have faith like that?* To that I'd say, Jesus said you have to have faith like a child. And with God all things are possible!

Around the same time that I got saved, my mother was diagnosed with pneumonia. Her illness kept her bedridden for a long time. Since most of my siblings had moved out, I had to learn how to fend for myself. This pushed me into survival mode. As a young girl, I learned to cook for myself, clean for myself, and take care of myself. I had to take care of myself when nobody else was around. But the truth is, it wasn't me. God kept me—even when I didn't know it. Experiencing God's faithfulness as a child helped me to trust him as an adult.

I survived some painful things as a child. Some memories were so painful that I blocked them out. But through the pain and struggle, I never let go of God, and I never let go of my song. God used my singing to draw me to him. I was so young, but God used my voice to save me from myself. He used this gift to protect me from the dangers of life. Whenever I sang "I Don't Feel No Ways Tired," I knew that a brighter day was coming—even through moments of darkness. It was instilled in my heart early on. I believed that God was going to use me beyond my wildest dreams. So, for as long as I can remember—from the time I was eight until right now—God's been building my faith, giving me a testimony to lean on when the road got rough and the going got tough. I knew God was for me and with me, even when I was alone.

Tough is a perfect word to describe how it felt to be a man without a father. Me? I was like a father for my younger brothers during a time when I needed a father myself. My oldest brother went to live with my grandparents, and since I was the oldest at home, I became the father figure. I was the disciplinarian. I was the example. But I also was a child.

Today, many people see me as an outgoing comedian and a social butterfly, but surprisingly I was very shy when I was growing up. I didn't talk much in class—my, how things have changed—and my teachers were so impressed by my behavior, I was named the good citizen of my school. That pretty much meant I was the best kid in my school.

When was that?! And how old were you—five?

You can't just say, "Congratulations," Tam? Always trying to steal a brotha's shine (LOL).

Sorry. Congratulations, Bae.

Thank you. That's better.

In fourth grade, I figured out that I could make people laugh, and it was downhill from there. They say people who like to make people laugh do so to keep from crying. In other words, most comedians entertain as a way to mask, hide, or use their pain for a greater purpose. That's what I did. I saw a lot of painful things in my home, and I channeled that pain into something helpful and useful. Ultimately, it made me the guy I am today. That's why I say every painful experience became a necessary ingredient for the life I wanted to live. Because my mom moved us around so much when I was a kid, I vowed to be a stable man. Because my dad was absent for my entire life, I vowed to be a present father. Because my mother was married three times—and each time the verbal and physical abuse got worse and worse—I vowed to be a committed, loving husband. All the painful experiences of my past helped me to become a better man in the future.

I felt like the moment I stopped would be the moment I failed.

That's something you need to know about me to understand me. I'm playful and fun, but when I commit, I'm in it to win it. Everything I did, even as a boy, I committed to it. If I played a sport, I was committed. I didn't let anything stop me. I felt like the moment I stopped would be the moment I failed. Like my mom, I kept going, no matter what.

DRAWN TO THE LIMELIGHT

During my years at O. D. Wyatt, I was pretty involved. I was on the football team and the track team, I sang in the choir, I was on the boxing team, and I was a member of the drama club. My mother was busy working three jobs at one time just to make ends meet, so she didn't have time to come to any of my games or my matches. I think in all four years that I played, my mother may have come to one football game and one boxing match. But she was frustrated and overwhelmed. I understand it now, but I didn't understand it back then. A lot of times my mother took her frustration out on us. Momma wasn't the nurturing type. She was the "if I have to say it one more time, I'm going to knock you out" type. She didn't have time to cuddle and hug us. She couldn't give us her undivided attention and affection.

I think that's why I learned to live for Friday nights in high school. The football field was where I got the attention and affirmation I wanted my mother to give, from fans and friends who came to see me play every week. I'm telling you, Friday nights were the best days of the week! Every Friday during football season my adrenaline ran high. I couldn't wait to get out there and play with my buddies Jessie Hurst, Cedric Smith, and Anthony Brooks, under the leadership of Coach Willie Chris.

Coach Chris was a major mentor to me in high school. He knew I didn't have a father in the home, so he treated me like his son. He didn't just teach me plays for the field—he taught me principles for life. He helped me to see my value beyond the sport I played, and he is one of the reasons I was able to push past my pain and find a greater purpose through it all. Coach Chris was a surrogate father to me, and to this very day, we still keep in contact. Coach Chris and my choir teacher, Jewel Kelly, were my saving graces—both sent by God to help me find my voice.

FINDING MY VOICE

Ms. Kelly *literally* helped me find my voice in chorus by giving me several opportunities to lead songs, despite my hesitation. I wasn't unfamiliar with singing. My mother was a phenomenal singer and musician. For years she led the choir and played the piano for our church, so with my mother's passion for music and Ms. Kelly's insistence on training me vocally, I now see how God was using each person to mold me in an area.

I never expected to make a career out of music. Soon I was singing in local groups and local choirs, and because of Ms. Kelly, I felt like I sounded pretty good. So good, in fact, that my buddy Cedric and I decided to start a little rock band. Looking back on it, we sucked. But we won a talent show in school that Tam attended. Right, Tam?

Right. And I'll never forget that talent show either. That was the show where you tore off your shirt to end your performance.

Yup, and come to think of it, that's when you fell in love with me.

No, sweetheart. Not true.

You don't have to act shy now. Just tell the truth, Momma. When you saw my strong, muscular hunk of a body underneath that shirt, it was love at first sight, wasn't it?

No, it wasn't love at first sight. I actually felt bad for you.

Why?

Because it wasn't good at all. But the audience loved you, so I figured, *If they like it . . . I love it.*

Well, if that wasn't the moment, how did it happen? How did we meet, and how did we fall in love?

I don't think we would've met or fallen in love if it wasn't for Nicole Jones.

CHAPTER 2

WILL YOU MARRY ME?

And Other Questions David Never Asked

Meeting you was fate, becoming your friend was a choice,
but falling in love with you was beyond my control.

—UNKNOWN

Nicole Jones was my best friend from church. She and I did everything together, so, of course, she knew I loved to sing. Nicole told me about this group of guys called the Humble Hearts who sang together. One guy was named Kirk Franklin, another guy was named Darrell Blair, and the final guy's name was David Mann. David and Nicole were classmates in high school, and one day she overheard them all singing around the piano in chorus class. She said, "My best friend can really sing too." David looked at her and said, "Well, if she can sing, bring her to school so we can hear her." Nicole agreed.

THE MATCHMAKER

Next thing I knew, Nicole had me riding up to the school with her to sing in front of these three strangers. I trusted Nicole, of course, and I loved to sing, but I didn't know who I was singing for. The whole idea made me a little nervous. But Nicole assured me that they were great singers, so I figured, *You only live once. Let's do it.* Nicole's grandmother drove us to the school to meet these guys. If I had never been invited to sing for the Humble Hearts, I would've never met David Mann.

LOVE AT FIRST LISTEN

The moment Tamela walked in, we sized her up. "She can't possibly sing as well as Nicole has been bragging about." She did have that "I can sing" look. You know, some people have the look. The way they carry themselves, they just look like they know how to sing. She had that look. But also she seemed really shy. So I greeted Nicole, and then Nicole introduced her friend to us. "Everybody, this is my best friend, Tamela Johnson." We responded in unison, "Hi, Tamela." And then we backed away from the piano to give her some space to sing.

When Tam opened her mouth, heaven met earth. She blew us away! I can't tell you what song she sang that day, but I can tell you that my mouth dropped open. Me and my boys, Kirk and Darrell, looked at each other on the sneak to see if the others were just as shocked. We were stunned. Her voice was so rich. Her tone was so distinct, and her range was out of this world. She sang difficult notes effortlessly. She didn't even appear to be nervous. All I kept thinking after she sang was, *Wooooah, this girl can really sing.*

To top it off, she sang that well by herself. I was confident singing

WILL YOU MARRY ME?

with a group, but I wasn't all that confident singing alone. Tam was an amazing soloist. She didn't need any accompaniment. After she finished, we thanked her for coming, and she thanked us for inviting her. We didn't have cell phones back then, so we didn't exchange numbers like we would now. I remember it was a Friday, and Tam mentioned that she was singing that night as a special guest for a church musical. We didn't have football or anything else going on, so we all agreed to go hear her.

TOGETHER ALL THE TIME

When they said yes to coming, I got nervous all over again. I felt comfortable with them in the choir room, but I was always a little nervous singing onstage for people who were listening to and watching every little thing I did. Sure enough, the Humble Hearts came that night to support me. I thought maybe I'd invite them to come to another musical I was in the next day, but wouldn't you know it, the Humble Hearts were already on that same program as me! They were singing at the same concert on Saturday.

From then on, it seemed like everywhere I turned, the Humble Hearts were there. David, Kirk, and Darrell were like the Three Stooges—you rarely saw one without the other two. I loved their tight-knit bond. I loved that they had each other's backs. And when they sang, I especially loved to hear that dark-skinned fella, David, sing the soprano note.

A PLAN TO SING TOGETHER

It wasn't a soprano note, Tam. I just took the high part to each song. Haha! It's all good, though.

15

Like Tam said, once we met, all four of us hit it off right away. Tam would sing on a program, and then we would sing on that same program. I remember she told us that we reminded her of The Temptations because we were energetic and very interactive with the audience. But Tam didn't need to interact with them. Her voice would stop crowds of people in Times Square if she started singing there. Man, this woman's voice was amazing! I decided I wanted her to be a part of our group. I just didn't know if she would be open to it. So the guys and I started plotting among ourselves.

After a few weeks of bumping into each other, I finally invited Tam to sit in on one of our rehearsals. I asked her if she would be interested in singing a tagline to one of our songs, and to my surprise she said yes. We gave her the song we wanted her to sing, and when she got to the rehearsal, we asked her to sing the part while one of us did the lead. She did it. Then we said, "Why don't you sing the lead, and we will back you up?" That was exactly what we wanted in the first place; we just didn't know if she would take the bait. She did! She'd already learned the entire song to rehearse with us, so we had another great suggestion: "Why don't you just come to our next gig and sing the song with us?" She said, "Okay."

Before you know it, people were comparing us to Gladys Knight & the Pips because Tam was leading and we were backing her up. Slowly but surely, we went from singing with each other to going out to eat, to hanging out with one another, to getting rides to and from work and enjoying each other's company on a regular basis. Tam became one of the fellas. It was three of us, but we treated her like one of the guys.

TRUST GROWS

Our friendship was everything to me. And when I say we were friends, I mean we were really friends. We spent a lot of time together. And David trusted me. He'd confide in me about the girls he was dating, and I confided in him about the guy that I was talking to. We both found each other attractive, I think, but that wasn't the focus in the beginning. I enjoyed being around him. I enjoyed talking to him. He made me laugh and, most important, he loved God. If it wasn't for our solid friendship, I don't know what we would've done when life got really hard. That's why I always try to encourage our children to build friendships before they date. Falling in love is all good, but one day, you're going to need more than a husband to hold you—you're going to need a friend who understands you. That's what David was for me from the start.

What I loved about David was that his love for me was effortless. He included me with the guys, but he didn't treat me like the guys. He was protective of me. He was mindful of me. He paid attention to things that made me uncomfortable. The guys were always playing around, but certain games he didn't let them play with me. I liked that about him. And he was honest. Even though he had several women who were interested in him at one time, he didn't lie to me. He told me the truth, and that transparency helped me to trust him.

> **He told me the truth, and that transparency helped me to trust him.**

TESTS OF A FRIENDSHIP

I trusted Tam too. I trusted her with my life. I trusted her with my secrets. And because we didn't do things for one another with an ulterior motive of sex, intimacy, or affection, it was easy to love her. Tam was one of the first people I told when I found out that I was going to be a dad. When I found out Porcia's mom was pregnant, I called Tam, and she helped me in every way. Tam became the intermediary between me and Porcia's mom to make sure that I could see Porcia when she was born. Tam stayed in the hospital with me while Porcia's mom was in labor to make sure that everything happened smoothly. I can't stress it enough—friendship is everything. Those hours we spent listening to one another, laughing with each other, and helping one another to reach our goals as teenagers—those were precious seeds that we cultivated into a wonderful garden of love.

As great as our friendship was, at some point we both started hinting that we were interested in being more than friends. I just didn't want to come on too strong because Tam was a different kind of woman. She was a woman of strength. She was a woman of standards. I wasn't going to play with her heart. If we were going to date, I had to do it right.

And David did do everything right until he kissed me. I was sitting there, just minding my business, and David kissed me and messed me up forever.

Now, Tam, don't you do that! Don't you play innocent like you didn't want me to kiss you!

I mean, I did want you to kiss me, and I did like you, but my older sister Charlotte always told me not to let a man know when you liked him. She said specifically, "If you like a boy, Tam, don't ever tell the boy you like him. Let him tell you first." So, that's what I did. I played the game until you couldn't resist me anymore!

Haha! Let me explain what really happened when we kissed for the first time. Tam and I were mentors for a young-adult community choir that we started with our friend Darrell. We were the oldest kids in the choir, and they looked to us for answers to simple questions. One day, we were riding in the van and the subject of how to kiss came up. Now I don't even know how or why we felt it important to demonstrate for these young people the perfect way to kiss, but that's what we did. We were sitting in the back seat of the van, and I said, "I'm going to teach y'all youngsters how to do it right. This is how you kiss a girl. You don't just run up on her and start kissing. You have to master the art of it. If you're going to kiss somebody, you have to kiss them like this."

I leaned over to Tam, planning to simply peck her on the lips. She leaned in toward me and responded differently to my peck. She pressed in, and I looked in her eyes, and they were misty.

I could tell she wanted more, but I played hard to get. Everyone on the van whispered, "Ooooh," as if they had been sneaking around to watch a movie they didn't have any business watching. I leaned in again to kiss her. This time our lips touched for more than three seconds, and next thing I knew, Tam stuck her tongue out!

Now, sir! Sir! Sir! First of all, you wanted me to tongue kiss you. Second of all, you were pressing in just as much as I was pressing in.

I mean, however you want to paint this picture, because you always tend to lie when it gets to this part of the story, I'm fine with it! The fact is, if Tam had not stuck her tongue out, it would've stopped at a peck. But all of a sudden, we were kissing for real. Then she got pregnant right there in the van, and we got fired.

David!

Okay. That's not how it happened. But that kiss confused so many people because everybody thought we were just friends.

We were friends. What people didn't know was we were attracted to each other.

Right. So for a while, we had been saying little things to each other, and I noticed how she would smile and blush. Then she would say things to me and I would flirt back. We had a little song that we listened to during that time called "Secret Lovers," by Atlantic Starr. It was this duet, and we would sing the lyrics back and forth. Nobody really knew what it meant to us, but it was a perfect song for us at the time:

> Secret Lovers that's what we are,
> we shouldn't be together
> But we can't let it go, oh no,
> cause we love each other so

Without question, we liked each other—and probably loved each other—but I wanted to take it slow. I had a few "extracurricular dating activities" going on. Tam also had a friend or two on the side—we'll get to that later—and I didn't want to add Tam to the number. I wanted to clean my slate and do it right.

Right. So, David and I had the kiss, but we didn't focus on that at the moment. We focused on being friends, singing, and learning about one another. A few months after our kiss, Porcia was born. That's when I felt my connection with David grow stronger.

Oh, it was strong all right. Soon Tam was inviting me over to her apartment. She and her friend Karen were roommates at the time. Every time I came over, another one of my favorite meals was added to the menu.

David.

Nope, don't "David" me. I've got a testimony and I'm going to tell it! Tam would have my favorite cereal waiting for me one week, then she would happen to be making my favorite meal—pork chops, rice, and gravy—on the night I was coming over after cosmetology school. It was very apparent that she wanted to sex me up.

David! You are too much! I won't agree to everything David is saying, but I will admit that I was very attracted to him at this point. I liked him, and I knew he liked me. David started sneaking over to my place, or he'd say he was "just in the neighborhood" and come over. Then he started asking me what-if questions, like, what if you had kids? How many would you want? Or what if you had to buy a home? When would you want to buy it?

THE TRUTH COMES OUT

Every question I asked her, she answered perfectly. Light bulbs started going off, and I really wanted to explicitly get her to admit her attraction for me, but the time never really presented itself. And then, once again, Nicole Jones stepped in.

One day, I had Porcia and we were taking her back home to her mom. Tam was driving, Nicole was in the passenger seat, and I was in the back seat with Porcia. All of a sudden, Nicole turned around and said, "You know this girl likes you, don't you? I mean, David, come on. She is helping you see about your baby, she feeds you, and she takes care of things for you. You know this girl likes you. Quit acting dumb!"

I wasn't dumb, but I wanted to play the game, so I said, "Tam and I are friends. I figured she did all of this because we have always been great friends."

Nicole was done with me. She said, "Don't be stupid. You know this girl really likes you."

David looked at me as if we were standing outside on a hot summer night under a fully lit midnight sky. "So you like me like that, huh?" he asked.

Shyly, I whispered, "Yeah."

I felt butterflies in my stomach. I was so glad to finally tell him how I really felt. A weight lifted off of my shoulders, and I felt free because I could tell he liked me too.

Thank God for Nicole Jones. She made me come to that school to sing. Then she made me tell David the truth in that car. But we didn't move into exclusive dating until I ended my relationship with my male friend, and until David ended his relationships with his girlfriends.

THROWING AWAY THE HO CARD

You just love to make it seem like you were the Virgin Mary and I was this reckless harlot! All right—I'll own it. I had played many games when I was young, but Tam made me man up. When I began to fall for her, I knew I had to throw away my "ho card." I knew I had to give it my all. And that's what I did. When she and I became official, I was all in. I didn't flirt. I didn't cheat. I didn't look at another woman inappropriately.

Several months went by, and people started making the connection that we were boyfriend and girlfriend. I knew it was time to ask her to marry me, but I didn't know how I was going to do it. I couldn't afford to buy a ring, so I borrowed one from my mom. How would I propose? I really didn't know. The truth is, I didn't have a plan. I just knew she was the one.

I knew I had to throw away my "ho card." I knew I had to give it my all. And that's what I did.

One day I was riding with her in the car. Tam was driving and I was in the passenger seat. I'll never forget it—we were exiting off the freeway on Collins and 20—and out of the blue, I blurted out, "We're going to get married."

He didn't get on one knee. He didn't ask me to marry him. He just told me, "We're getting married." After he said it, we just kept riding, and we talked about something else until we got home.

How awkward, right?! Tam heard me propose, and she never addressed it. She never said no. She never said yes. She said nothing—for three long weeks!

Finally, I brought it up again. I said, "Hey, did you hear me? I said we are going to get married."

She said, "Yeah, I heard you." Then she went back to cleaning.

"Well, why didn't you say anything?" I asked.

She just stared at me like I had two heads while I sat there waiting for an answer.

I heard David ask me the first time, but I wanted to be sure that he was going to be committed to me and me alone. Even though he had broken up with the girls from his past and even though he was pulling away from all those other girls, I needed to be sure. I wasn't about to get played the way I saw him play others. But when he showed me he was serious, I agreed to marry him.

COMMITMENT

And that's how it happened. No bells. No whistles. No Facebook announcement. No engagement party. She said, "Okay," and we started thinking about when and where it would all happen. When we got engaged (if you want to call it that), most of our family and friends were surprised because they only knew us to be close friends. Tam was staying over a lot more than usual. Well, one day, Tam and her roommate had a falling out, and Tam ended up with nowhere to live. All of her belongings were in her car. I didn't notice at first when she came over to spend the night. When I finally asked her, she told me about their disagreement and how she had moved out. So, I went to my momma and asked if Tam could stay with us. She was already basically a part of our family, and she didn't have anywhere else to go. To my surprise, my mom agreed. A few days later Tam moved in.

It was a major adjustment to have Tam under the same roof as my mom and my brothers. As a houseful of guys, we were used to doing guy things. Plus my mother wasn't too fond of the idea of Tam staying there at first. She always had something to complain about—*Tam is too loud. Tam is too neat.* But eventually, she fell in love with her. We had so much fun.

Yeah. We had a little too much fun if you ask me.

Why do you say that, Tam?

Because our "fun" led to me getting pregnant!

CHAPTER 3

A BABY ON THE WAY

The littlest feet make the biggest footprints in our hearts.
—UNKNOWN

Pregnant? I can't be pregnant. I couldn't believe it. We had just decided to get married and now I was pregnant? When we conceived our son, we were living at David's house with his mom and brothers. Late one night, while everyone else was asleep, David and I decided to sneak and "play house." We started doing what only grown, married people should be doing and got caught up in the moment. I think both of us knew I was pregnant after that night. I was just in denial.

"I CAN'T BE PREGNANT!"

Oh, I knew for sure you were pregnant because I know my skill set! All jokes aside, when Tam and I found out we were pregnant, it was the best of times and the worst of times.

I agree. I was working at a nursing home. David was trying to build his clientele as a hairstylist. We both wanted to get our own apartment, but we couldn't afford the rent on our income alone. So David asked his oldest brother, Darrel, if he wanted to share an apartment with us, and he agreed. In addition to doing hair, he and Darrel were driving trucks for a senior-citizen food service. I wanted to work with them, so I put in my two weeks' notice. I had planned to quit my job in Richland Hills. The only thing is, the new job required me to take a physical. Part of that physical included X-rays of my back. I didn't want to get an X-ray because I knew in my heart I was pregnant (even though I didn't have confirmation of it yet). How did I know, you ask? Well, one morning, after eating breakfast, I went to the cafeteria area to clean tables, and next thing I knew, I was vomiting up my breakfast. I was still working at the nursing home, but I felt awful. I knew I couldn't keep putting it off, so I told David that we had to go to the doctor to see if I was truly pregnant.

The drive to the doctor's office was awkward and quiet. Both Tam and I were nervous about the results, but I was excited at the same time. I knew she would be a big star someday, so I wanted to trap her—just kidding! But in all honesty, I knew I was going to marry Tam; I just didn't expect it to happen like this. When I looked at her during that slow ride to the doctor, I knew what she was thinking.

WHAT WILL PEOPLE SAY?

I was thinking, *What am I going to tell my momma?* I couldn't think about anything else. I knew she would be crushed to find out I was pregnant out of wedlock. My siblings and my mother—especially my mother—had certain expectations of me. They were always concerned about what people would say. I was always told to be on my best behavior. As a Christian girl from the South, the rules were simple: Be seen, not heard. Be respectful and polite. Smile and pray. Pray and smile. Most of all, don't have sex until you get married.

I knew my mother would be disappointed, but on top of that, I wondered, *What would my church family think? What would the young adults from the community choir think? How would I explain myself to strangers in the supermarket when I started showing? And WHY IS DAVID DRIVING SO SLOWLY? Hurry up already!* It was torture—knowing before you know, but waiting to find out what you already know. And even though I knew, I was kind of hoping it wasn't true.

I was hoping for the exact opposite. I wanted Tam to be pregnant; we just had a lot of loose ends to tie up. In my mind we were going to be together anyway, so I wasn't worried. We knew what we were doing. Besides, we knew how we got here. The night David Jr. was conceived, Tam had looked at me and said, "I think I'm going to get pregnant from this." She felt it in her heart, but she also had done the math. She'd been ovulating. She'd counted back to the exact day, and like most ladies, she knew the window of opportunity for a probable pregnancy. My mind-set was, "Well, if this is the window, I'm going to plant a seed."

David!

Sorry. Back to the drive. Finally, we pulled up to the clinic. Tam went inside and I waited for her in the car. I can't remember why I didn't go inside with her—perhaps there was no parking, or maybe she wanted to go alone. I waited in the car with joyful anticipation. Tam was hoping she wasn't pregnant. I was hoping she was. The suspense was killing me. I tried to listen to music, but nothing good was on the radio. I cranked up the car to feel the air conditioner. It got too cold. I turned off the car and let down the window. The sun made it too hot. I looked up to see every woman walk in and out of the door. Tam seemed to be taking forever.

Finally, when she walked out, she looked like a zombie. She didn't blink. She didn't smile. She had no expression on her face. She opened the door, slid into the car, and sat there with a blank stare. Silence. Unbearable silence.

Then she said it. Looking straight ahead (and not in my direction), she murmured, while trying to hold back her tears, "I'm pregnant."

I yelled, "*Yesss!* Cool!"

She said, "Nooooo, not cool."

ALTAR CALL

I figured everything would work itself out. By the time she found out she was actually pregnant, we had an apartment—so on that end we were secure. But in Tam's mind, everything was happening too fast. We'd thought Tam would get that job working with me, so she'd quit her nursing home job, but then she didn't. Now she was home 24/7, living with me, and, still, we weren't married. On top of that, she was pregnant.

The way Tam and I grew up, that was a *no-no*. We couldn't be singing praises to God every Sunday, traveling around town to minister to others, when we ourselves were still "shacking." We had to do something quick, so I suggested we go downtown to the courthouse and get a marriage license. At the time, we needed twenty-four dol-lars to do it, and we didn't even know where that was going to come from. But somehow we scraped up the money to get our license.

A week later, we went to church on Sunday morning and walked down to the altar together. The altar call in our church was a moment that usually happened after the sermon. Normally, people who felt they had sinned would come to the altar to repent and ask for for-giveness. Every time the church doors opened, Tam and I would go to the altar to repent because she was pregnant and we were living together. In our minds, we had to go to the altar each week to secure our salvation.

This Sunday was a different Sunday for me, though. I was tired of repenting. I was tired of asking for forgiveness. I didn't want to go to the altar anymore, because I knew we would go back home and continue in our "life of sin." So, I looked at David and said, "We need to just get married." He said okay. We had done the legal part already. We had already gotten the marriage license, but we needed someone to facilitate the ceremony. We couldn't afford a wedding, so I suggested to David that we ask our pastor, Sherman Allen, to do the ceremony after the service. He agreed.

So we did it right then and there, on that Sunday afternoon. Most everyone had left church, but there were about ten friends and family members remaining, lingering inside. We walked over to ask if they would be witnesses to our wedding, and they said yes. David's mom was there. Our friend Darrell Blair was also there. Pastor Allen conducted the ceremony, and even though my momma lived down the street from the church, I didn't ask her to come. I knew she would be happy for me, but I didn't want my strong dislike for my momma's third husband at the time to ruin my day. I just wanted to clear my conscience and say yes to the man of my dreams. In front of ten family members and friends, David and I said "I do" on April 24, 1988. At last, I was at peace in my soul.

I was at peace, too, because when we got home, the experience was sweeter than honey in a honeycomb!

Lord, help my husband! Even though he's right—it was sweet—I was just so glad to call him "husband." From that day on, I didn't feel guilty anymore, like God was going to get me. And the fear of dying in my sleep went away. I was living according to God's Word, and for me, that meant the world. But I know my story isn't every woman's story. When some people get pregnant outside of marriage, they feel pressure to marry someone they don't love. I get it. Maybe they get married just because they want their child to be raised in a two-parent home. But if those people having a child aren't in love, then I strongly feel that marriage isn't the best option. Marriage is not something anyone should rush into or feel pressured to jump into.

> **I was living according to God's Word, and for me, that meant the world.**

I can certainly speak to that from experience. Porcia's mom and I had our daughter, but we weren't ready for marriage and all that came along with it. We both love our daughter, and we never wanted her to feel as if *she* was a mistake—God doesn't make mistakes. But her mom and I had jumped the gun and done things out of order. As adults, we took responsibility for our actions. Sometimes the best thing you can do to ensure the health and well-being of your child is to choose not to marry. Again, I'm a man who commits wholeheartedly. The way I saw it, if I couldn't say, "Forever," then I couldn't say, "I do." And if I couldn't say that I would be willing to die for this person, then I couldn't say, "I do." I was sure I loved Tam. I knew I would give my life for her, so marrying her was easy.

LIVING AS A MARRIED COUPLE

The moment we said, "I do," the next thing we were focused on was making sure Tam delivered without complications. And, of course, we wanted to walk with the Lord together.

We'd been attending my home church, Shiloh, led by Pastor Sherman Allen. After we married, we decided to go to Tam's uncle's church—Holy Tabernacle Church of God in Christ. Her uncle's church was also amazing. We appreciated the preaching there, and we connected with many people as well. But over time, we both agreed that we needed to find a church where both of us could be comfortable. So we set out to figure out who would be our collective pastor, as husband and wife.

In 1988, our son, David Jr., was born. He was a good baby for the most part. In the beginning, he woke up every hour or two, but we were so excited to have a child, it didn't bother us. What we didn't expect was that Tam would get pregnant less than a year later with Tia. David Jr. and Tia are eighteen months apart. The moment we got our rhythm with one baby, we had another one and had to start all over again.

I knew my body and I knew when I could get pregnant. But somehow, my cycle got messed up after David was born. When I officially learned I was pregnant with Tia, I was already four months pregnant. I knew something wasn't right because I had been sick like this only one other time before—when I was pregnant with David. This time, though, I was working at Pearle Express (Optix) and my friend Regina heard me complain about being sick in the morning before work. She asked if I was pregnant. So I went to the drugstore and purchased a pregnancy test. It came back positive.

Somehow my pregnancy with Tia seemed to go faster than David's. And, of course, since we had a baby already, we were focused on him and not on having another one, but it happened. My cravings were different too. My cravings with David included spicy foods like picante sauce or jalapenos. But when I was pregnant with Tia, I only wanted Mexican food, and I only wanted it from this one particular Mexican restaurant called Tia's.

When I looked at the sign one day, I said to myself, "I ought to have a baby with a name that begins with the letter T. Maybe it should begin or end with a T—I don't know, but I do know I want a T in her name." And when Tia was born, there was no other name that fit her but Tia, the name of that Mexican restaurant.

What's funny is that Tia loves eating Mexican food to this very day.

It's true. So now we had Porcia, David Jr., and Tia. Thank God our niece Sonya was there in the house to help us take care of our babies. But how Sonya came to live with us is a dramatic story.

My sister Lea Ella (we called her Teeny) had five children. A few years before she turned thirty, Teeny was shot in the head by an ex-boyfriend. This left her crippled both physically and mentally, and her daughter Sonya nursed her back to health. It wasn't perfect, but they were managing. Then Teeny discovered she had cervical cancer—terminal. Before my sister turned thirty-one years old, she had passed away, leaving her five children behind.

Sonya was a warrior. She had helped her mom cope with her illness until she passed away. When she needed somewhere to go, David and I offered our home to her. We took her in as our own, even though we were twenty-two-year-old newlyweds. She was fourteen years old at the time.

Needless to say, the house was filling up pretty fast. Very quickly, David and I had to adjust to so many things happening all at once. David Jr. was starting to talk. He was calm, but he was sneaky. Baby Tia cried all the time. Sonya had lost her mom, and, as a teenager, she had her own share of mischief that we had to deal with. As for me and David, it seemed like we just couldn't stop arguing! Every little thing caused us to argue. But soon enough, I figured out why I was so irritable. I was sad a lot more than usual. I felt overwhelmed by life. I didn't eat much, and I was always grumpy about something. Every time Tia cried, I took it personally. I knew God had blessed me with a beautiful baby girl, but it just seemed like she didn't like me. Whenever I held her, she would cry. If I put her on my chest, she cried. But the moment David picked her up, she would stop crying.

So I went back to the doctor and explained my symptoms. He diagnosed me with postpartum depression.

No doubt, that chapter in our lives was chaotic. The babies came. Sonya came. Tam's mom came. I'm proud to say that we survived those first few years of marriage, and we were really finding a level of balance between working, feeding, living, sharing, and loving. Tam and I were together, raising a full house, and, together, nothing could stop us.

And then . . . the doorbell rang.

CHAPTER 4

KNOCK, KNOCK!

A Surprise at the Door

*As much as you want to plan your life, it has a
way of surprising you with unexpected things
that will make you happier than you originally
planned. That's what you call . . . God's Will.*

—UNKNOWN

Life is full of surprises. Some surprises are good. Some surprises
are not so good. But God is good, and he works all surprises
together for our good.

Five years into our marriage, a surprise that almost messed up
everything came knocking on the door. At the time, life was pretty
good. Tam and I had gone from singing occasionally while we worked
other jobs to singing as a career with Kirk Franklin and the Family.
We were helping each other build our careers. We had finally gotten
through the rough stages of early marriage (or so we thought), and

we were doing all right. I had learned her likes and dislikes. She had learned to adjust to the reality that she wasn't single anymore. I had learned not to make major decisions without including her. She had learned not to spend whatever she wanted to spend without accountability and communication. We had left diapers behind, and we had two preschoolers and a teenager. It was all good in the Mann household. Until someone knocked on my door and told me, "Surprise! You have another child!"

Served? What do you mean I've been served? If I've been served, where are the mashed potatoes and chicken wings?

Oh, you read that correctly. No need to go back and read it again. The surprise of all surprises showed up five years into our marriage by way of a constable knocking on my door. He handed me some papers and said with a stern voice, "Mr. Mann, you've been served."

Served? What do you mean I've been served? If I've been served, where are the mashed potatoes and chicken wings? Where are the collard greens and yams?

The constable wasn't playing with me. This was not a joke. He had come to my home to hand-deliver papers informing me of two things:

1. I had a child.
2. I possibly owed child support for a child I didn't know was mine until a few minutes ago!

Now, waaait a minute. Tam and I had just gotten our careers off the ground. We were just beginning to grow as parents. We were growing as a married couple, and now this! I looked at that paper as if it were a jail sentence. That's honestly what it felt like. I had been faithful to Tam during our marriage. This child had been conceived before we ever said "I do"! My past was haunting me. My sins were catching up with me. The first thing I thought was the same thing most men might've thought: *This child ain't mine!*

Denial was easier than accepting responsibility. I was scared. I was shocked. I knew I'd gotten married with a lot of baggage, and I knew I had dated a few women before Tam, but I didn't think in a million years that life would throw me this kind of curveball. With hands trembling and a mind so blank you could've written the entire Bible on my brain, I closed the door and stood there for about five minutes. I said nothing. I did nothing. I just stood there.

I needed a plan. I needed to weigh my options. What could I do to guarantee this news would be received in the easiest way possible?

Option 1: Don't say anything to Tam. That's it! I figured it out. I wasn't going to say anything to her. Instead, I'd take a paternity test and keep the results to myself. And if I found out the child wasn't my child, all would be well in the Mann house. It would be my little secret. But if it turned out she was my child, then I would figure out my next steps.

It was a perfect plan until I realized that my secret would eat me up inside. How long would it take to get the results? How long could I keep this from Tam? How long could I walk around the house as if everything was perfectly fine—knowing that things were *not* fine! Besides, my wife would know something was wrong. She's always had this intuitive thing about her. I couldn't keep a secret from her even if I tried. So I quickly talked myself out of Option 1.

Then I tried to think through the best way to break the news to her. After all, it wasn't the easiest conversation to have. How do you break it to your wife that you have a five-year-old child you just found out about?

Enter wife.

Tam: Hey, baby.

David: Hey, Momma.

Tam: How was your day?

David: My day was good, baby. How was yours? What did
you have for lunch? Oh, by the way, I have another child!

Nope. That wasn't going to work.

I needed another plan. I had already brought one child into our marriage, and I knew that Tam was not fond of baby mama drama. I also knew enough about Tam to know that this conversation was a face-to-face one, so I waited until she got home. I heard the car drive up into the driveway. My hands started sweating. I heard the key turn in the keyhole. I ran to the bathroom to throw some water on my face. After a few minutes of awkward silence, I walked into our bedroom and said, "This girl done filed child support against me!" Tam looked at me, and all I could see on her face was . . . pain.

WHAT TAMELA *REALLY* THOUGHT

David thought I was in pain. But the truth is, I was in shock. Imagine what it must've been like to be me that day. There I was—minding my own business, doing my regular duties for the day—thinking about what I was going to cook for dinner and totally not expecting what David was about to say.

I remember it like it was yesterday. I had just come home from work. I was ready to relax before the busy weekend. We were singing every weekend at that point. The phone never stopped ringing—thank you, Lord! I was grateful for the opportunities and the doors God was opening, but I also loved being home with my family. I loved the peace that came over me when I stepped into our house. Imagine how nonpeaceful it felt that day when David told me that some other woman was suing him for child support, for a child I didn't know he had!

At the core of my pain was betrayal. I was caught off guard. I felt like David had lied to me—even though he later explained that he really didn't know the other woman was pregnant. I didn't process all of that until later. All I could think about at the time was where I fit into the equation.

Who was I to him?

Who would I be to them?

What would our life look like now?

We were already at capacity. My mom was living with us. Sonya was living with us. If this child was his, David would have to take care of four children now, by three different baby mamas—where was I on his list? How would I factor into this situation?

On top of all that, I was angry. I was angry because I felt like we were being punished for not getting married the right way. Somehow, a guilty heart will find every reason to condemn itself. Looking back, I know I was taking on unnecessary blame and pain for something I didn't do and something I didn't cause. But that was my baggage. For years I'd seen my mother do the same thing. She took on pain that she didn't inflict and apologized for things she didn't do. When my sister was abused by her boyfriends, I saw her arguing and screaming at men who didn't respect her when she should have just walked away. I saw her make extreme sacrifices for guys who never said thank you. This was a part of my bloodline. Most of the women in my family carried the weight of other people's problems.

Maybe that isn't a Johnson family problem. Maybe it's a human problem. Maybe all of us share the same pain of guilt and shame, of overthinking and regret—of listing our mistakes more than we count our blessings.

Everything you could think of, I thought of it in that moment. But I knew, deep down, that everything would be all right. I had been through difficult seasons before, and I knew without a doubt God would bring me out of this one. I used to tell my friends, "Don't panic! Don't lose focus. Take a deep breath, pray, and trust God to work it out." Easy advice to give; not so easy to take.

Maybe all of us share the same pain of guilt and shame, of overthinking and regret—of listing our mistakes more than we count our blessings.

When I finally mustered up the strength to tell David how all of this made me feel, I told him the raw truth. Another baby mama fueled my insecurity. I knew that none of our children were a mistake, but I didn't think my life would look like this. I thought I would get married, have kids, and love one man for the rest of my life. The problem is, the man I loved had children before we got married, and then we had a child before we experienced life as a newlywed couple. I worried that somehow I would get lost in all of this. The kids would take priority. The other mothers would be calling and interrupting our family rhythm. Somehow, David might stop caring about me. And then he wouldn't treat me the way he had been treating me.

I now know that my insecurities were all a result of what I had been exposed to in my own home. David wasn't my father. David wasn't my stepfather. David was David. And if I was going to love him, then I needed to trust him. When David heard my heart, he reassured me by reiterating our vows. His reassurance changed my entire perspective.

He sat me down and took my hand gently in his. Then he whispered in the most loving way, "Momma, you are my priority. Everything else revolves around you." He told me that no matter what happened in life, we would get through it together. That was the only option. There was no other choice on the table but for us to do this together. He included me in his joy. He included me in his sorrow. He included me in his plans. He didn't make me feel like an afterthought. He helped me to understand that I was a blessing, not a burden. And then he uttered these words that have stayed with me until this very day. He said, "Tam, it's *us against the world.*"

CHAPTER 5

CHASING OUR DREAMS

Working Toward Our Goals Together

*Anniversaries are days to celebrate the love
that makes your marriage great.*

—UNKNOWN

The first years of our marriage were tough. What could have been a deal breaker between Tam and me ended up making our relationship even stronger. We were truly getting to know each other as husband and wife and trying our best to build a better life for our kids than we had growing up. Knowing we had this unshakable trust and love binding us, Tam and I were a force! And somehow having a super-blended family worked well for us. Sure, it was challenging working our regular jobs, traveling, and singing a lot with Kirk Franklin and the Family. But the more time Tam and I spent doing life together, the more we began to get the hang of love and marriage.

That doesn't mean it was easy. Oh, no. It wasn't easy by any stretch of the imagination. Our first ten years were the "struggling years." Financially, we struggled to make ends meet. We struggled to budget and balance our lives. And we struggled because we really wanted to have something that we could call our own.

DREAM HOME

I wanted to make Tam as happy as possible, and the moment she said she wanted something, her desires became my new project. I was so obsessed with making her happy that I forgot all about budgeting and timelines. All I knew was that Tam wanted a home, and every day we'd drive by this one house that Tam's mom used to clean when Tam was a child.

That house was big and beautiful with white columns in the front. When we were younger, we thought it was a humongous house, but it wasn't that big, quite honestly. It just felt that way compared to how we lived.

Tam would always talk about how beautiful that house was, and she told me she dreamed of living in a really nice house. So I stretched our finances as much as I could to buy a house similar to that house she'd loved growing up. I stayed up late and I woke up early to help with the construction and wiring of the house. I didn't let other people labor to build it. I wanted to put in the time and labor to make sure it was perfect. I was willing to do anything that my wife needed in order to make her dream come true.

In marriage I think a lot of people lose their will to fight. I think a lot of people become accustomed to the way things are, and they make sacrifices in the beginning that are not always sustained during the difficult seasons. Anyone who has been married for a long time can confirm that the foundation should be built before other things steal your concentration away from your marriage. Now, I don't have any regrets, but if I could've done things differently, I would've tried my best to have a vision for our family *before* we had children. I would've also paused to really come up with a solid financial plan. A lot of the strain and stress of our marriage, in the beginning, happened because I lost sight of the big picture. I was so eager to give Tam what she wanted immediately. My intentions were good, but if I had been thinking long term, I would've saved us both a lot of headache and heartache.

DREAMY HUSBAND

I will say that David wooed me with that house. He worked his tail off. And once it was finished, it was beautiful. I was so proud of David and so happy. That was the best gift he ever gave me. The best gift anybody ever gave me.

Ah, Momma. That makes me smile.

But the bad news is, by the time we got the house, I was so exhausted with making her dream come true that I ended up passing out after the first week of living in it. I literally fell out. I had to go to the doctor because I was exhausted, and I hadn't even made my first mortgage payment! That experience taught me to really take my time before making a major investment. Yes, I could provide for my wife, and that was great, but I forgot we had to eat the next day after we moved in—and that wasn't so great. I had put the cart before the horse. I needed to keep my eyes focused on long-term goals so I

I needed to keep my eyes focused on long-term goals so I wouldn't be sidetracked by temporary needs or wants.

wouldn't be sidetracked by temporary needs or wants. We wanted our marriage to succeed, so Tam and I would need to learn to press pause on the temporary to establish a plan to secure us for the long haul.

We were growing up in so many ways. Learning together. That's what life is all about: learning. Now, remember, we were still pretty young. We'd married at twenty-one, so by this point we had a houseful and we weren't even thirty! All of the kids were in school. Tia and David were in elementary school. Tiffany was in school for the performing arts. My niece Sonya had moved out. (That's a story for another time.) And Porcia was living with us too. David and Porcia's mom never went to court to decide about custody; everyone just agreed it would be best for Porcia to live with us, so she moved in. She was in middle school when she officially came to live with us. I was working as an optometrist at Pearle Express. And on top of that, David and I were singing with Kirk Franklin and the Family. Life was full.

Life was good, but life was very hectic! Tam and I were on a high because we were traveling the world at someone else's expense. Singing was Tam's passion, and this was something we always wanted to do: travel together, worship together, and raise our children together. We were seeing all our dreams come true!

We wouldn't have said this at the time, but now I know we were allowing life to drive us without really driving our life. We lived on the edge of our seats, waiting for the next opportunity. Plans weren't solid. The children were our anchor. But we didn't really know what was next. We just kept going—working, spending, and loving—until one day, the phone rang.

CHANGE OF PLANS

It was Kirk Franklin and the management team. They said, "We want to talk to you both if possible. Can you make yourselves available for a lunch meeting?" *Sure, we can do that.*

Now remember, we had grown up with Kirk. I had traveled with him since we were young. We agreed to meet for lunch, eat some great food, and talk about whatever he had on his mind.

At lunch Kirk told us something we didn't expect. "Look," he said, "I think I'm going to take a sabbatical and do away with the Family."

We looked at each other and said, "What do you mean *do away with the Family and go on sabbatical*?" We didn't even know what a sabbatical was. By the end of that meeting, we learned though. Kirk planned to end our group, Kirk Franklin and the Family, and pursue a different musical path. He wanted to try something different.

Well, congratulations, Kirk! More power to you! We were happy for him and his new chapter because he was our friend, but I was dumbfounded. What did this mean for our family? We had just purchased a home, and singing each weekend with Kirk helped to pay the mortgage. What were we going to do now?

In one hour, we went from the highest high (buying a house, traveling the world, and loving it) to the lowest of low. How was I going to take care of my family? I'd been working with Kirk full-time. I was no longer doing hair. I was doing plays with Kirk, recording with Kirk, and my life and livelihood revolved around the success of Kirk

Franklin and the Family. I couldn't say I was mad at him. But I can say I was nervous about our financial future.

DAVID FINDS A NEW OPPORTUNITY

Let me tell it to you straight. David had quit his other job. He didn't have a clue what we were going to do to pay the bills for our big family. When we were in town, I still continued working at Pearle Express. David, though, was desperate to figure something out. His desperation ended up leading him into an opportunity. David decided to call one of the promoters who had worked with us while we were singing with Kirk Franklin on the last play we had done. That was the key that unlocked a great door.

The promoter told me he was only promoting plays at this point, but he had a tip for me. He said I should meet a playwright and director having auditions for a new show in Chicago. That was all he needed to say. I calculated my frequent flyer miles and used everything I had to go to Chicago to meet with this guy.

When I got there, I didn't know what to expect really, but they brought me into a building, and when I opened the doors, there stood a tall dude with a huge head. (LOL, I know he will call me when he reads this.) He was directing several people. That guy was Tyler Perry. It was one of his first plays, and I was there to audition for him.

During the audition I said, "If you choose me to work with you, I would be honored to come. But my wife and I are a package deal. She doesn't act, but she certainly sings." Tyler agreed and gave Tam and me a chance at acting in his first stage play, *I Can Do Bad All by Myself.* In that play the characters Mr. Brown and Cora were introduced to the world, alongside another character named Madea.

Nobody knew what we were doing with these characters. Nobody knew us in Chicago or anywhere else outside of Fort Worth, Texas. A celebrity actor was supposed to join the show. Tyler was expecting that person to be the main draw for this play. But for whatever reason, that individual didn't show up the first night. We had fun, and the audience loved it. We figured the next night the celebrity actor was going to arrive and we'd get back to the plan. But that individual didn't come on the second night either. So Tyler Perry brought all of us actors together and split the lines between us. "You take these lines, I'll take those lines, and we'll make it work." On opening night, we got away with it. By the second night we were nervous. We thought we would get booed off the stage. But instead of booing, the crowd got bigger and bigger every night. Even though the celebrity actor never came, people filled the theater night after night after night!

By the fourth night, no one was looking for or asking about that celebrity actor. Next thing we knew, we were selling out at the Regal Theater in Chicago. Word on the street was, "We love Mr. Brown and Cora." Nobody knew who we were, but they loved these characters. They loved Madea, they loved Mr. Brown, and they loved Cora. Tam would sing, and people would give her a standing ovation. I would act, and people would laugh until they cried. That first play changed the direction of our lives forever.

SUPPORTING EACH OTHER'S DREAMS

After we finished touring the play, we came home and asked ourselves, "What's next?" Tyler wanted me to do another play but was unsure of how David would feel about me going by myself. David was extremely supportive because he knew I loved to sing. And I was excited about the opportunity. So I went out on the road again, this time to do a play called *The Diary of a Mad Black Woman*. I played a character named Myrtle.

David's support meant the world to me. He was always the voice I leaned on for direction, and when he gave me the green light, I felt like I could accomplish anything. Having a husband as a support system and as a cheerleader is an amazing gift because when the lights, camera, and action went away, I knew I had a man who was willing to do anything to make my dreams come true.

> **When the lights, camera, and action went away, I knew I had a man who was willing to do anything to make my dreams come true.**

When Tam left for Chicago to act in her second play, I stayed in Fort Worth to take care of the kids. Our roles switched completely, and before I knew it, I was Mr. Mom. I figured I could handle it. I kept asking myself, how hard could it be? Just fix a few meals. Wash a few loads of clothes. Drive them to school, and for the rest of the day, let them play until they go to bed, right? Wrong! It was one of the hardest jobs I have ever had. Getting the kids ready for school was easy because they dressed themselves. Picking them up from school and taking them to practice or that friend's house wasn't bad. But the hardest part was going to the grocery store. It was just too many items. If all I had to buy was one loaf of bread, I would be okay. But there were so many different brands of everything! Some days, I would be in the store for hours at a time. I would select the brand that I recognized, but it was also the most expensive choice in the aisle. I had no sense of what groceries cost either. So, if we needed milk, I would give Porcia forty dollars to buy a gallon of milk, and she'd look at me strange but not say a word. She knew I didn't know how much a gallon of milk cost because Tam did all of the shopping. I didn't know what to get and how much to buy, so while Tam was on the road, I would call her in a panic and ask, "Which one do I buy? This brand or that brand?" And she would chuckle and say, "*Bae*, just pick one."

Our roles had certainly reversed. Tam was the breadwinner, and I was the one taking care of the home. Like a lot of people, guys especially, I tended to put my value on how much I was contributing to our home (in terms of money). But this experience changed that. I wasn't working a conventional job, but I was doing full-time work as a "domestic technician." This was a full-time job! Going to soccer practice, track practice, football practice—and everybody was in sports. Cleaning, washing, lifting, hugging, asking, "How was your day?" over and over and over and over again! I needed a raise, but I didn't know where to apply for one. I did a lot of things well, but I wasn't the best washer.

You were an okay washer.

I knew how to separate the colors at least. But she's picking on me! Tam, all of us don't have the woman superpowers to do it all well and still look wonderful while doing it. But I do remember washing something in hot water that needed to be in cold water. That didn't work out too well because I accidentally shrank all the clothes I washed!

Yes, that was right before I went to New York—the same week as 9/11.

Absolutely. On top of trying to be superdad, Tam was on her way to New York when the terrorists attacked on 9/11. That morning I turned on the television and saw news of two planes crashing into the Twin Towers. I panicked. Tam was scheduled to travel, but I didn't know for sure where she was that day. All I knew was that she wasn't home, and I was a nervous wreck until I heard her voice.

David called me that morning and said in the calmest voice he could muster, "Do you see what's happening on the news?"

I responded, "No, what's happening?"

He screamed, "Terrorists just blew up the World Trade Center! Did you guys get to New York yet?"

I said, "No, we haven't gotten there yet. We're supposed to leave for New York in the morning."

I can't describe the peace that came over my entire mind, body, and soul when I heard Tam's voice. Tam and the other cast members were scheduled to travel to New York by plane. But so many airports were shut down that they changed plans. They took a bus from Detroit to New York.

Back in Fort Worth, I was so nervous that I went to the store and filled our car with bottles of water. Everybody around me thought this was nuclear warfare; I thought this just might be the end of the world. I went and picked up the kids from school early. I don't know why—I just wanted to be close to my children. The kids didn't understand what was going on. They were just excited to be out of school. I had the perfect plan. I was going to gas up my red Ford F-150 and drive to New York City to pick Tam up. The drive would take twenty-four hours from Texas, but I was determined. I told her, "Just relax. Sit tight." The next morning I woke up determined to drive north to pick up my wife.

But after I spoke to Tam and heard in her voice that she was all right, we decided to wait so that I wouldn't put myself in danger too.

The cast and I finally arrived in Manhattan after that long drive from Detroit. It was so gloomy. The sky was still smoky. It was the weirdest feeling. The city that was usually so full and lively felt so empty and quiet.

The hotel where we were staying didn't have room service, so in order to have lunch we needed to leave the premises to get food. When I told people I was going out to the store, they looked at me as if I was crazy. "Are you sure?" they asked. They were scared, but I couldn't sit in the hotel room and starve to death. At some point I had to get something to eat. I wore a hospital mask to protect myself from the smoke in the air. It was a terrifying feeling. It's sad to think about it even now, but I'm so glad I had a man who would do anything to rescue me. He was willing to drive nonstop from Texas to New York to take care of me. That day I fell in love with David all over again.

FINDING OUR RHYTHM

If I had to pinpoint the primary lessons we learned in our first ten years of marriage, I would say we learned the importance of foundation and flexibility. We had always shared a deep love for God, and our faith was an important foundation, but those first ten years helped us to figure out a rhythm that worked for us. We stopped comparing our needs to those of other friends who were also married, because few people could identify with our story. Not many of our friends traveled, managed a super-blended family, and dealt with the unpredictability of toddlers, teenagers, and other life challenges.

Our lives were already fast paced, and we had no clue what was about to happen to our careers. We were learning to be flexible. We threw out the traditional roles of what a man should do and what a woman should do, and we decided to be a true team. If food wasn't on the table, I figured out how to make it happen. If bills needed to be paid and for whatever reason I didn't earn money that week, Tam figured out how to make it happen. Our gift to ourselves, after ten years of marriage, was the freedom to be David and Tam without trying to compete with or compare our lives to anyone else's. And that, my friends, was the best gift we could've ever received.

CHAPTER 6

FAME

Figuring It Out

*Fame doesn't fulfill you. It warms you a
bit, but that warmth is temporary.*

—MARILYN MONROE

If the first ten years of our marriage taught us about foundation and flexibility, then the next ten years taught us how to make better decisions. Year by year, Tam and I learned how to make better decisions that always put our family first. We learned how to trust God for the unknown, and we learned how to believe in each other.

Thanks be to God, our career had taken a major shift. More and more people were taking notice of us. The plays were becoming pretty popular. Strangers would walk right up to us and talk like we were their biological family members. I knew something was different when Tam and I would be driving down the road and we would see copies of our plays being sold as bootleg DVDs. Or we would be heading to the theater to see a movie we were in, and people would be selling the movie illegally right in front of us! To me, that meant people around the country were beginning to notice us. But fame means nothing if you are not happy and whole inside. I'm so glad my wife became the barometer for success and not the applause or silence of people. When she smiled, I knew I had succeeded. And that was all I needed to keep going.

The moment our success clicked for me was around 2006 when *Meet the Browns* became an actual television show. It was amazing to see people from our hometown stop us and greet us at the airport, but when people from different countries and nationalities stopped us in the airport to say, "Are you David and Tamela Mann?" it was a whole other level. It was exciting on the one hand. On the other hand, it was frightening. I had no idea that people would know our names one day. I didn't have a clue that the plays and movies would resonate with so many people. Fame had never been the goal. Even now, even till this day, David and I see ourselves as regular people. We love to laugh. We love to sing. We love to talk. Quite simply we just *love* to *love*. We don't see ourselves as celebrities; we are just grateful that God has given us multiple platforms to spread joy and faith.

> David and I see ourselves as regular people. We love to laugh. We love to sing. We love to talk. Quite simply we just *love* to *love*.

This journey has strengthened our partnership, and it has also taught us about the importance of maintaining humility. Many of our friends have gotten caught up in the hype of people asking for autographs and pictures, but I believe Tam and I were able to remain centered because we never confused the blessing with the Blesser. It's God who opens these doors for us. It's God who makes all things happen for us. We have always had God, and we have always had faith. Plus we have a family that reminds us every day that the trash still needs to be taken out, the light bill still has to be paid, and a grandkid's recital is coming up that we can't miss.

WEAKNESS AS STRENGTH

My insecurities also helped me to manage the shift that happened in David's and my life. I know that might sound strange to hear, but I believe God used my insecurities to keep me humble. Because I never saw myself as this great vocalist or as this amazing person, humility came naturally for me. Even in this industry, where many times business executives are either trying to tell you that you're greater than you are or criticizing you about what you aren't doing right, our faith was central to keeping us balanced, but our truth kept us centered. I didn't go to college. That was the truth. I wasn't the best singer. That was the truth. I was made fun of for being overweight. That was the truth. But somehow God still allowed me to touch people's lives.

Our life is a miracle. I will never take it for granted, and I have vowed to always be regular ole Tam. If you ask me where I learned it from, I will point to Jesus. Jesus was the Savior of the world, and at the same time he was a servant. To me, it doesn't get any better than that. From Jesus I learned how to manage the highs and lows of the industry—because one day people may be saying, "Congratulations," and the next day they may be saying, "Crucify them."

Absolutely. You want to talk about humility? Children are good at keeping you humble! I'll never forget the time we all went to see Tia play basketball at her school. I was there as Dad. Tam was there as Mom. But the people saw "singers, actors, and celebrities," so they stopped us as we were rooting for Tia and asked to take pictures with us while the game was going on. We didn't think anything of it, so we took a few pictures, and then, out of the corner of my eye, I saw Tia's face of disappointment. She literally stopped playing in the middle of her game and said, "Are you not going to watch? Is this what you both came here to do? Are you really going to take pictures with everybody while my game is going on?"

That was a humbling moment. I felt so scolded and rebuked by my own child. But she was right. It was difficult to hear at the time, but I'm so glad she spoke the truth. We wanted to make sure our supporters knew how important they were to us, but we didn't want our family to feel forsaken. When Tam and I learned how to manage the criticism and balance our family time and marriage time, it made all the difference.

BALANCING LIFE AND WORK

This was a major struggle for us. We wanted to attend every game. We wanted to show up at every concert. We wanted to respond to every engagement request, but we couldn't do it all. We were living out our dreams onstage, but we were missing out on so much at home.

Whether it was a basketball or football game, a track meet or just simply being there for our kids—we were missing out. If we are completely honest, when our careers were taking off, our family life suffered. Our time was limited. Our energy was limited. Our funds were limited, so we couldn't just hop on a plane every time something was happening. We had to make the best decision that worked for as many people as possible.

Thank God our children were understanding. They knew we weren't traveling mindlessly. They understood we were working, but every mother and father knows what it's like to carry work guilt with them everywhere they go. If they aren't feeling guilty because they couldn't attend the PTA meeting, then they feel guilty for working too many hours. If they aren't working too many hours, then they feel guilty because they can't afford a family vacation. Guilt can easily rob you of joy if you allow it to. But Tam and I were

> **Every mother and father knows what it's like to carry work guilt with them everywhere they go.**

determined to self-correct whenever we realized we were making the wrong decision. We weren't afraid to apologize to our family if we hurt their feelings unintentionally.

I can only imagine what it was like being a kid in high school during all of this. While we were experiencing a whirlwind, our children were affected by it as well. They wanted us present, but they knew we had to make a living. The tension was definitely real, and for a moment it seemed like a major divide. David was emotionally worn out some days because his passion for parenting is greater than any other man I know. David Jr. had always played football (from peewee to high school), and David had to miss a lot of his high school games. But I'd watch David listening in by phone—getting the play-by-play from his brother. I watched his excitement when David Jr. made a tackle and won the game.

And I saw his disappointment when David Jr. lost a game. He brought all of that onto the stage, each and every night. He didn't talk about it a lot, but I knew he missed being there for his son.

And not just David Jr., but Tia, Tiffany, Porcia, and Sonya. Tia was a state champion powerlifter. Porcia was running track, Tiffany was paving her acting career, and Sonya was beginning a family of her own. Like every family, children want their parents home with them all of the time. And, of course, they tend to get in trouble when their parents are out of town.

One time David Jr. was acting up so much in school that I called him while we were on the road, and I said, "Look, if another teacher calls me about your behavior, I'm going to fly home and talk to you face-to-face." Of course, David Jr. didn't believe me, and he continued acting out. So I hopped on a plane after one of our shows, and when he woke up the next morning for school, I was on the couch looking at him. He was nervous. He was shocked. He knew he was in trouble.

I knew I couldn't stay long. When I went to reprimand David Jr., he said, "So you can come home when I'm in trouble, but you can't come home to see me play football?" I didn't expect those words to come from his mouth, but he was admitting his truth. Perhaps he was acting out to get my attention. Perhaps he was doing things to make me come home.

Certainly our children were worth the trip. They were everything to us, and this was only one of the costs to fame. But it was a high cost.

QUALITY TIME

The other cost was the absence of time to just rest, relax, and recharge. We didn't have time for breaks because we didn't have a traditional nine to five. As soon as one opportunity ended, we were preparing for the next. Sometimes we were ending one project and starting another at the same time. Sometimes we didn't know if the script we were holding was from a play ending or a movie beginning. We just had to learn how to balance those things together—to say no if it caused too much strain on my family and to unplug when we were having family time so that all of our children knew how important they were to us.

When it came to quality time between David and me, it was difficult at first. David and I saw each other every day, but work was work. Business was business. We quickly learned how important it was to get away with the family once a year and then to get away and spend time with each other once a year. Vacations are a refueling station for us. Even if we are around each other 24/7, we still have to make quality time a priority—because quantity doesn't equal quality.

Now that we have learned our lesson, there are some things we will never do again. We will never put an opportunity over and above our children. We will never neglect our times of rest and replenishment. Thankfully our children are now a part of our team, but even if they weren't, we are more realistic about what we can do and what we can't do. I am a living witness that when your priorities are right, everything else will fall in line.

CHAPTER 7

THE MANNS GO IT ALONE

Finding Courage in Each Other

You face your greatest opposition when
you're closest to your biggest miracle.

—BISHOP T. D. JAKES

Whenever God wants to take you to the next level, God will bring people into your life that will give you the courage to do so. That's exactly what happened to David and me. While we were on the road with Tyler Perry, acting and singing for another play called *Madea's Family Reunion*, David had a grand idea (he's famous for those).

"Let's go in the studio and start recording some songs," he said.

Songs? As in, me singing by myself? Oh, no. I wasn't ready for that. I appreciated David's support, but I wasn't ready to make that move. What do I look like—an artist? Artists have to do so much more than sing. They have to take a lot of pictures. They have to be strong communicators. They have to encourage the crowd. I can't do all of that. I'm sorry, babe. I'm just not ready.

A LITTLE PUSH

The truth is, Tam was ready. She just needed an extra push. That's what we've been for each other. When I thought I was at the end of my creative rope, Tam would push me to go back to the drawing board. In fact, countless times she had pushed me to further my career in acting, and I was so grateful that I wanted to return the favor. To me, that's what marriage is all about—partnership and pushing.

I see in Tam what she doesn't see in herself, and she sees in me what I don't see in myself. Tam was committed to doing plays (because that was my passion), but that wasn't hers. Singing was her passion, and I felt like it was the right time to spotlight my wife's amazing voice.

I cannot tell you how many arguments spiraled out of this recommendation. Who would've thought that my desire for Tam to become a solo artist would cause a problem in our home? In her mind, she wasn't good enough to lead. She was a great background singer, but leading wasn't her forte. This was all in her mind. I knew something different. The world knew something different.

Isn't it interesting that sometimes we are the last person to see the greatness that is in us and on us? I looked at my beautiful wife, and I told her, "Honey, you are a world-class singer. You not only have the gift to do it alone, you have the anointing to bring the gospel to the world through song." When she didn't take my word for it, God started bringing people into our lives to confirm what I already knew was true.

ENCOURAGERS

Around the same time that David was pressing me to do my first solo project, we were still singing and touring with Kirk Franklin and the Family. This was in the early 1990s. At one of our tour stops, I ran into CeCe Winans, and somehow CeCe and I began talking about my solo project David was excited about.

I told her that I was scared to do it. She asked me why. I felt so comfortable talking to her because her presence was so calming. Seriously, every time she spoke, it seemed like a host of angels just followed her and sang in perfect harmony around her. When she listened to my concerns, she said, "I used to be scared too, but do what God has called you to do." CeCe had spent years singing alongside her brother, so she knew what it was like to step out and begin a successful solo career. I could trust her; she knew what she was talking about.

A few months after that, we were invited to sing with Kirk Franklin and the Family for Natalie Cole's Christmas concert at the Wilshire Theatre. It was a star-studded event. What a night! President Ford, Tim McGraw, former first lady Hillary Clinton, and Wynonna Judd were all there. While I was sitting in the dressing room, Wynonna Judd walked over to me, and we began to engage in small talk. The music project came up again, and I told her my concerns. She listened to everything I said, and then she responded, "Just do it, Tam! Do what God called you to do."

I said to her, "But I don't talk like others talk."

Then Wynonna sternly said to me something I will never forget. She said, "The Lord didn't call you to talk. He called you to sing. If you do what God called you to do, the rest will come naturally." Wynonna understood my other concerns (about image and weight), and she was fearless in her advice. I believe God sent those two women to me to give me the final push I needed to make my decision. After praying about it, I finally told David that I would do it.

SOLO ALBUM

But nothing in our lives happens that easily. Once Tam agreed, we went into the studio as soon as we could. I wrote a few songs, and some of our friends wrote songs as well. Tam sounded great. The music was coming together. It was powerful. We named our first project *Gotta Keep Moving*, and it was a perfect way to describe our lives during that time. No matter what we faced, we decided to keep moving. Even when unexpected twists and turns happened, we had to keep moving. We wanted to encourage others to do the same—trust in God and keep moving.

No matter what we faced, we decided to keep moving.

We released the project independently, and we were so happy with the sound and quality that we decided to record a live version of the studio project. We knew nothing about live recordings. We knew nothing about managing a label. But we decided to trust God all the way, and that's what we did. I asked a close friend to invest in the project, and he agreed. Altogether our budget for that recording was sixty thousand dollars! This was the largest investment we had made at the time, but we were trusting God all the way. We filed the paperwork for our label. We came up with the name Tillymann because Tilly is Tia's nickname, and Mann is our last name. We thought it had a nice ring to it.

We spent weeks preparing for this live recording. This would be the moment that would change everything. We got busy arranging the performance we would record as *The Live Experience.* We'd done a lot of production by that point and a good bit of recording. But this was a whole other level—an elaborate undertaking with an orchestra, lighting, staging, backups, the works. And because we'd be recording *live* it was even more crazy.

On the night of the recording, everything went wrong! The camera crew dropped several balls. The fog machine we ordered for special effects weighed about five hundred pounds, and we didn't have anyone to help us bring the machine inside. All I kept thinking was, *We've invested sixty thousand into this recording. We have to make it work.* And then the unthinkable happened. I walked over to Tam during the sound check and her voice was gone! She rarely gets hoarse, but that day she had nothing vocally to give.

VOICE FROM ABOVE

I was literally drinking blessed oil on the night before my recording, hoping and praying that God would perform a miracle. I didn't know why we experienced so much opposition, but then again, I do. Any time something great is about to happen, often conflict shows up with it. Whenever David and I experience great levels of opposition, we know God is going to bless us in a major way. And I can't tell you what happened, but all I know is that when the first song played and I had to sing those notes, my voice came back miraculously. The crowd was amazed, my children were smiling from ear to ear, and David was in tears. He had heard me struggling to sing all week long, and he knew that only the Lord could do a miracle like this.

I can honestly say that our first live recording was one of my most memorable live experiences with Tam. She hit notes she had never hit before. We sensed the presence of the Lord. And the audience loved it! We knew that something was definitely about to change. And change it did! Once that first recording happened, everything else started falling into place. Tam's songs got played on the radio. We started releasing project after project after project. After *Gotta Keep Moving* and *The Live Experience*, we released *The Master Plan*, *Best Days*, and *One Way*—the album that earned Tam her first Grammy award as a solo artist!

As the music world began to embrace Tamela Mann as a solo artist, television producers started to send in offers and scripts for us as well. *Meet the Browns. Mann and Wife. It's a Mann's World*—all of these became TV shows. Movie offers started coming in as well! Some days we would leave the studio after singing, run on set for our reality show, and then have a production meeting for our movie shoot the following week. Not only that, but God really started showing off. We began producing the shows that we had once acted in, and at one point so many offers were coming in that we had to turn a few opportunities down. We had learned our lesson from before—not to pile on too much and lose focus of our family—so we tried our best to accept the blessings but choose wisely.

With each opportunity, Tam and I grew to love one another even more. We began to meet even more celebrities and A-list actors, but that only increased our appreciation to God for the many blessings he had given us. Our hard work began to pay off. We rarely left each other's side. We woke up together. Went to work together. Read lines together. Walked down red carpets together. Edited shows together. It became a 24/7 marital partnership for real!

24/7 PARTNERS

I know. I know. Most people would *never* recommend working with their spouse 24/7, but for us it has been the greatest decision we've ever made. Tam and I decided to depend on each other more than we depended on strangers. We removed the training wheels from our careers and trusted God and prayed about everything together. As we stepped out in faith and started to go it alone, God began to blow our minds. Our children began to work with us. Most times they got fired and rehired several times over. But we saw everything coming together. We had our high days and our low days—we still do. We had our days of major disagreement,

We woke up together. Went to work together. Read lines together. Walked down red carpets together. Edited shows together. It became a 24/7 marital partnership for real!

but no matter what, I always knew she had my back. Over time we learned how to step away for a moment and process our feelings, but in the end I fought for her and she fought for me.

To those who are afraid of stepping out and trusting God, I want to encourage you to do it afraid. Maybe you don't feel good enough, smart enough, or talented enough, but do it afraid. I know there are a few obstacles in your way, but do it afraid. God is faithful to blow your mind if you just trust him and believe in him all the way.

Thank God I have a husband who was determined to see me win. Thank God I have a family who supports their momma's dreams. I know without a doubt in my mind that none of this music success would've happened if it weren't for David Mann.

I had to learn to trust God but also trust the people God sent into my life. Some days, I was shaking in my boots, but David's words would come back to me. And I'd remember CeCe's and Wynonna's encouragement. I remembered my mother's constant encouragement. I remembered my friends from high school telling me that they were proud of me. I remember my first solo in church, and the countless people who walked up to me and said, "Thank you for letting God use you." With each door God opens now, I am amazed at his power.

I know without a shadow of a doubt that, with God, all things are possible. For me those words are more than a saying in my life. It is the motto I live by. I am no longer afraid to try anything. Acting, directing, singing, dancing—bring it on. With a strong support system, and with my hubby by my side, I am positive that everything that God has for us is within our reach—if only we have the faith to believe it.

CHAPTER 8

EMPTY NESTING

Just Us Now and It Feels So Good

*All of a sudden, the nest is empty. The birds have gone,
and what had been a constant blur of activity is now
nothing more than a few discarded feathers. Silence
mutes all that was colorful and it is time to reestablish
our significant place in an ever-changing world.*

—MARCI SEITHER

Tam grew up in a big family. I did too. And when we married, it
was never just the two of us. It was three, then four, then five—
from almost the moment we said, "I do," we had children in the oven
and children at the doorstep. We had extended family living with us,
and we were the village babysitters for other families in our neighborhood. Our life has always been noisy. If the babies weren't crying,
then the television was blasting. If the phone wasn't ringing, then
somebody was burning something in the kitchen. Then one day we

looked up and our kids were grown. Now none of them live with us anymore.

When Tam and I realized we were approaching thirty years of marriage, it shocked us. Where did all the time go? How did that happen so fast? We'd been having so much fun that we didn't realize how much time had flown by. Life has always moved quickly for us.

But I'm going to be honest with you. Silence? It's the best sound in the world now. The only thing we may hear is the dog barking, but other than that, when we turn the key and enter into our home, we hear that beautiful sound of silence. It wasn't always this way, and we loved it when it wasn't, but it has become a beautiful blessing.

David and I never planned to be empty nesters. Our dream world would have included our entire family living in a large mansion where every child had their own wing for their kids and grandkids. We would come downstairs, eat dinner together, and go on with life as usual. We've always loved to be with our family. But our family didn't always love to be with us!

EVICTION NOTICE

Some of our kids wanted to leave the nest quicker than others. Porcia was ready to go. Sonya was out the door. Tiffany and Tia weren't quite ready to leave, so we had to force them out. But I did it cleverly. You see, I didn't have many rules in our home, but one rule I was strict about was keeping their bedrooms clean. Tiffany and Tia found that rule impossible to obey, so I told them once. Then I told them twice. Finally, after I straightened it up for them one final time, I warned them: "Girls, if I walk back in

this house and your room is a mess, you will be asked to leave."
Problem is, they didn't believe me.

So when I saw their rooms looking like a war zone, I was done.
I had had enough of asking two grown women to clean their
rooms. They weren't getting the picture, so I created the picture
for them. I had David write an eviction notice and tape it to their
doors. The eviction notice said something like, "EVICTED effective TODAY. Please vacate the premises immediately."

**Actually, you hired me to do your dirty work, and the kids thought
it was my idea. So they got upset with me when they got home. You
were somewhere singing, "Take Me to the King."**

David, hush! This is what really happened. When the kids got
home, they were shocked. I will never forget the look on Tia's
face. "Are y'all kidding?" she asked.

I responded, "No, I'm not kidding. By the way, did you read
the fine print at the bottom, which says that you are to vacate the
premises immediately?" I explained to both girls that they had
not kept their end of the bargain, and we had reached a fork in
the road. I'm sure they thought I was crazy, but I was as serious
as a heart attack.

Tia, always the baby and dramatic one, stormed into her room
and started cleaning up. Tiffany, on the other hand, gave a very
philosophical response. "Well, if that is the reason I'm being put
out, then I'll just leave."

**I told her she didn't have to get all jazzy and try that reverse psy-
chology on us. If she was going to go, then she needed to just go.**

Those were some hard conversations. As parents, Tam and I

always required our children to honor and respect us. Our disciplinary actions weren't random—they resulted from the kids' neglect and unthoughtful behavior. I told them they had to leave, but honestly, my feelings were hurt. Tam and I were making this decision as a team, but I hated to think they were mad at me. I don't know why everybody thinks of Tam as the angelic host and me as the mean guy—the truth is I'm the angel! Tam would've evicted her kids and started smoking weed in their room the next day.

David!

Well, maybe not weed, but certainly Newport cigarettes—if she smoked. I'm joking! Tam is a beautiful soul—everybody knows that—but she also knows how to put her foot down. Me, on the other hand, I'm softhearted. I was the parent who let the kids back in. I hired them back again after we'd fired them and said, "You get one more chance." Tam wasn't to be played with. When she has had enough, she's done. And the only way they could change her mind was to come back in the name of "Daddy said."

So that's how the girls left. David Jr. took his time moving out. He dragged his feet because I think he liked being with his momma and daddy. But eventually he started his own family, and he had kids of his own to deal with. So the whole empty-nest thing kind of felt like it snuck up on us.

All those years together as a couple, we'd planned for family. We planned to buy our first home so we could all be together. We planned every birthday and graduation together. But we didn't plan for the day when our kids wouldn't live with us anymore. The silence is good now, but in the beginning it was eerie. I didn't know how to live in a house without noise. All our lives, we had taken care of someone. Suddenly there was nobody who needed taking care of.

When I was a kid, I took care of my brothers. When I got married, I took care of Tam and the babies. There was never a time when I wasn't providing for and protecting someone I loved. I must've asked Tam a million times, "Who are we going to take care of now?" And Tam gave the best answer that a wife could ever give: "We're going to take care of each other."

That's exactly what I said, and I meant it. We've lived a blessed life and accomplished so much. But one of the greatest achievements of my life is that I still like the man I married thirty years ago. I like the way he smells. I like the way he looks. He still gives me butterflies, and I enjoy being around him. To me, he is still the funniest man in the world. David's heart is so big, he would give everything he had to someone he loved in a heartbeat. That's the man I fell in love with, and that's the man I want to live the rest of my life with.

He still gives me butterflies, and I enjoy being around him. To me, he is still the funniest man in the world.

What happens in some marriages is that couples who fell in love with each other get caught up in taking care of the kids and providing for them. Then, when the kids leave, the marriage leaves with them. It's unfortunate because we all can become distracted with the routines, the shopping lists, the pickups and drop-offs, and lose track of who we are together—just the two of us. David and I have survived because our marriage was a priority over everything. I never had to reintroduce myself to him because, over the years, we continued to work on our friendship. My heart breaks for spouses who have become roommates or strangers. My prayer is that God will help every marriage to maintain their friendship and keep their fire going so that when the chapters change, their love will only grow stronger.

Now that we have more time to be with one another and to take care of one another, our marriage has reached a new peak. We enjoy talking to other married couples and helping them to communicate better and rekindle the flame. We've always loved traveling together, but now we don't just want to travel for work. We travel for play. We have learned to date all over again. We have learned to put more time into learning one another instead of splitting our focus on other things.

We also have learned how to take out our trash again, find the remote again, and walk the dog again. When our children left, our help left too! We used to trick the kids into cleaning up by telling them they were the greatest cleaner of them all. Of course, because they wanted to carry that badge of honor, they would work hard to maintain their gold medal, and we would come home to a clean house every week.

I had enough tricks to open up a store! One time, I told the kids to race to the mailbox to see who could get the mail the fastest. They didn't know I was actually too tired to go and get it myself, so I turned it into an activity—and it worked! Not only did they get the mail that day, but every day they wanted to race again and again. I think that's where the Mann competitions came from, because everything in our home was a big project or a big game.

But then, all of a sudden, no more monkeys were jumping on the bed. No more 2:00 a.m. curfews where the kids would wait until 1:59 a.m. to slide their key in the door. At first, it made me sad. But then it made me glad. Finally, I could have Tam to myself.

The empty nest made us appreciate the holidays a little more too. Thanksgiving and Christmas became "the Mann family reunion" for us, and we were able to cherish our memories with everyone when they came home. You know, it's funny—you never know how much you miss the noise until it's gone.

You never know how much you enjoy parenting your children until they are not there for you to parent anymore.

And you never know how much you enjoy parenting your children until they are not there for you to parent anymore. We became parents so young that it was always part of our existence, so we took it for granted. Sure, we will always parent our children for the rest of our lives, but the way they need us has changed. How they ask for advice is different. How they receive our suggestions is different. And how we pray for them has changed as well.

I want our children to have healthy marriages. I want our children to not repeat the same mistakes we made. I want to protect them from harm and help lead them in the right path. But sometimes you have to let go and let God. Even as David and I learn to love one another in this stage of our marriage, I'm learning to let go and let God.

NEW SEASONS

I'm still in love, and he's still in love. But what our love looks like is so different than it was when we were younger. We still work on our marriage, but what we work on is different because we're different. Now that David helped me step into my solo singing career, I'm dreaming even more. I now want to own a clothing line for women. I want women of all shapes and sizes to feel beautiful as they are. I want David to do comedy and entertainment all around the world. I want to see his name in lights, and I want to see him take home an Oscar. I want to make memories with David and leave a legacy for our children that helps them to see how you can rise above any problem and survive any storm. Life is still busy, but our goals are simpler. At the end of the day, we just want to love the Lord, love each other, and love our family.

PART 2

WHAT WE'VE LEARNED ALONG THE WAY

CHAPTER 9

COMMITTED TO *US*

Our Marriage Is Our Priority

*Love is not maximum emotion. Love
is maximum commitment.*
—SINCLAIR B. FERGUSON

It was a cold winter evening. A dark and stormy night.

Okay, maybe it wasn't dark or stormy, but it was certainly cold.

It was the dead of winter. David Jr. was only a few months old. We walked in the house, flipped on the lights, and nothing happened. I looked at Tam. Tam looked at me. I closed my eyes and thought, *Oh no, the light bill!*

I went outside to see if everyone else's lights were off too. I hadn't paid the bill—I knew it—but Tam didn't know it. So I walked around in shock as if a power outage had hit our entire complex. Why do we do that? Why do we go through the motions of shock by looking to see if something is wrong with someone else's house, knowing all along our lights are off due to nonpayment? I'll tell you why I did it. I was embarrassed. I felt worthless. I felt like I was less than a man. I started beating myself up and saying things in my head like, *What kind of man are you? You call yourself a man, but you can't even keep the bills paid in your own house?* It was a hypersensitive moment for me. I didn't know what to do or say to my wife.

Tam lit a candle and looked at me. I braced myself for the worst. She turned toward David Jr. and gently wrapped up our son in a warm blanket.

Then she said, "We have two options: we can go to your mom's house for the night or we can just go to bed. It's already late, and we don't need any lights to have a good night's sleep." By the time she walked over to me, I was weeping on the side of the bed. But she wrapped her arms around me and said, "Let's just go to sleep. We'll fix it tomorrow."

As we lay in the bed with warm blankets wrapped around us, I thought to myself, *Wow, if she can be this encouraging while I have her in the dark, just think how she will treat me when I am able to do better.*

As a woman, I know my man. I know when he's embarrassed. I know when he's ashamed. I know when he's tired. I know when he's angry. That night, David was already feeling defeated. It made no sense to belittle him and make matters worse. I vowed to be with him through it all, and I vowed to support him during his low points as well as his high points. The way I see it, life will always throw a lot of unexpected situations our way. I had a choice. I could make the best of it, or I could make the worst of it. I chose to make the best of it.

I never knew what God had in store for us back then, but today I can say with humble gratitude that God can do the impossible if you just trust him. Thirty years later, David makes sure we have plenty of lights in the house (way too many, if you ask me). Thirty years later, he has made every little wish I've ever had come true. I'm a witness that God will truly give you the desire of your heart when you commit to God and commit to your spouse.

I made a commitment to David, and there was nothing that could stop my commitment—no matter what.

COMMITTED TO OUR VOWS

The first commitment David and I made when we got married was to honor our vows. If we honored our vows, then divorce would never be an option. Within the first week of our marriage, we decided to remove the option of divorce from the table. We wanted each other to know "I'm not leaving you." We were accustomed to rejection, and we grew up in families where marriage was not as healthy as it could've been. We saw dysfunctional relationships, and neither of us wanted that for our lives. So we threw divorce off the table and focused on our commitments. We decided: if we do this, we are going to do this 'til death do us part. That was my promise to him. That was his promise to me.

You may be reading this having filed for divorce in the past, or you may be going through a divorce right now. David and I believe in the power of marriage, and we have committed to staying together forever. But in cases of abuse and violence, we do not condone staying in a marriage when you feel unsafe. If you find yourself in harm's way, get out. Abuse is never okay, and it is never okay to subject yourself to abuse. Please do not misunderstand that fact. In our case, for David and me, we wanted to remove the option of divorce because we both needed security.

Tam and I get asked all the time, "How have you stayed married for so long?" My simple answer is, God plus commitment. We committed to God first, and we committed to one another second. It's no secret.

Marriage has been on the decline in America for quite some time. One of the reasons people do not stay married is because wedding vows are not taken seriously anymore. A vow is a promise. These aren't just pretty words; they're your sworn vow. At one time the vows were the highlight of the wedding. At our wedding the vows were pretty much the whole ceremony because it was so spontaneous. But the vows traditionally were the most important part of the service. When vows were spoken, people paid attention. The room grew still. Hearts were opened. People were reminded of the beauty and sanctity of marriage, and the honor it is to conjoin one's life to the heart and hand of another . . . until death do us part.

But over time the wedding ceremony has changed. The vows have now become something to breeze by, upstaged by all kinds of other things: the twenty bridesmaids, the horse and carriage, the expensive dress and reception, and let's not forget the wild bachelor parties. Don't get me wrong! All of these things are wonderful if the bride and groom decide to have them. But as Tam and I raise our daughters (who are preparing to be brides themselves), one thing we always say to them is, "Don't spend so much time planning the wedding that you forget to prepare for the marriage." Marriage is a beautiful gift, but it is also a commitment. Anyone can fall in love, but marriage takes work. A wedding ceremony will last for one hour, but a marriage will last for a lifetime. When it comes to my life, it's Christ, it's Tam, and then everything else. Nothing has equal weight to my marriage because I am committed to this beautiful queen. When I looked into her eyes thirty years ago, I said these words to her:

> I, David, take you, Tamela,
> To hold from this day forward,
> For better or for worse,
> For richer or for poorer,
> In sickness and in health,
> To love and to cherish,
> From this day forward,
> Till death do us part.

Every now and then, I revisit my vows to make sure I am honoring my commitment. Journey with me as I explain what each stanza of my vows means to me.

I, David, take you, Tamela—That means flaws and all, I'll take it! I'm honored to serve her. I'm honored to bring her into safe habitation with me.

Have you ever gone to an auction and seen something on display that you wanted to purchase? No matter how high the price went up, when you saw what you desired, you screamed out in joyful jubilation, "I'll take it!" That's how I view my wife. Tam belongs to God, but God leased her to me. When Tamela offered her

> Don't spend so much time planning the wedding that you forget to prepare for the marriage.

hand in marriage, I accepted every part of her. I learned to love the difficult parts. I decided to take her *as* she was, but not leave her *how* she was when I met her. I discovered that my job as her husband was to regularly remind her of her beauty, strength, wisdom, and value. I learned very quickly that as the husband takes the wife to the next level, the wife will do the same for her husband.

To hold from this day forward—The word *hold* means "to cling to." The same way someone holds on to a banister when they are walking up a steep incline, and the same way someone clings to the safety bars on a roller coaster, so, too, do I cling to my spouse. The tighter the hold, the stronger the bond.

I saw my mother mistreated by men who didn't value her, and I realized from that experience how *not* to treat my wife. The worst kind of love is one in which a spouse feels emotionally homeless. I saw couples in church who lived together but did not love together. I had aunts and uncles who existed under the same roof, but there was no holding, no loving, no joy, and no enjoyment. I refused to let that be our story. Instead I committed to hold Tam from the first day I kissed my bride until now.

Tam taught me that sometimes the greatest form of intimacy is holding each other. As my wife, she wants to know that I can simply hold her. She wants to know that I will always prioritize her in the midst of demanding work hours, distracting voices, and difficult seasons. As her husband, I want the same thing. I want to know that she can hold my hand through it all. In the courtroom, the boardroom, the bedroom, I want to be sure that she can hold me forever. Why? Because thriving relationships don't just love each other; they hold each other.

For better or for worse—I once heard Oprah say, "Lots of people want to ride with you in the limo, but what you want is someone who will take the bus with you when the limo breaks down." This is the heart behind this vow for me. When I married Tam, I committed to love her for better or for worse. It's really easy to love on payday. It's easy to love when the checks clear. But when there was five dollars between the two of us, we still chose to love each other. When the bottom fell out, we still chose to love each other.

Tam and I are experiencing some great blessings these days. God has truly been good to us, but this road has been paved with many nights of uncertainty. Remember, I could barely keep the lights on when David Jr. was a baby. But now I have made sure she has more lights than she will ever need. She is the light of my house. She is the heartbeat that keeps me moving. When I vowed to love her for better or for worse, it never felt like worse to me. We just kept loving until things got better.

For richer or for poorer—This vow is not just about monetary wealth. It's also about the state of one's soul. Some days, Tam has felt like a million dollars. And it's easy to love someone who has courage, joy, resilience, and hope. Other days, Tam has felt bankrupt and defeated. I've seen her mount the stage to sing in pain all throughout her body. I've watched her struggle through laryngitis and somehow still minister to thousands through song. I've also seen her cry so much after several loved ones died that I didn't know what to do. My job as her spouse has been to love her out of her poverty-stricken state. I vow to love her until she feels rich even if she is poor. This vow is my commitment to be strength where she is weak so she can be strength where I am weak.

As couples climb the ladder of success together, it's so important to stay a team. It only works when you do it together. Often marriages crumble when success hits because the foundation of said marriage was not built on the solid rock of friendship.

In sickness and in health—One of the most difficult things to endure is when the doctor gives your spouse an unfavorable report. But one of the best things in the world is to not be alone while you get that news. Sometimes your spouse doesn't need you to fix it; they just need you to be present. They need you to hold their hand, wipe their eyes, read the medicine label, serve the food, tuck them in, kiss them on the cheek, and tell them, "It's going to be all right." Tam and I know this firsthand. In our time together we've had health challenges and unexpected situations with our children, but we've always gone through it all together. One of the greatest acts of love is to care for someone while they are sick. One of the greatest rewards is to watch them get better. One day, you may get a call that none of us want to receive. But today, you can sow seeds into your future to make sure your spouse has the best life they've ever had.

To love and to cherish—To love is to honor, adore, commit to, trust, and respect. To cherish is to esteem above all others. To cherish is to value with unique care. I value Tam like she is expensive china. Have you ever purchased expensive china? When you take it out of the box, you have to be careful about how you touch it. When you transport it from place to place, you wrap it up in protective boxes so that it doesn't get damaged. In the same way, my spouse is unique and special. I cherish her. I handle her with care. I aim to love her every day like it's the last time I'll get to show how much she means to me. I am committed to love. I refuse to let our love die. In that commitment to love I vow to listen more, talk less, hold more, and argue less.

In the same way, I want to encourage you to appreciate your spouse. Tell the world about your love for each other often and frequently. Your love can inspire others to see the world differently. Don't hide it under a bushel. Share it with the world, but most importantly, enjoy one another when no one is watching.

From this day forward—It's amazing that this stanza is in our vows twice. It's said in the beginning of the vows and at the end of the vows because from this day forward, to me, means *Tam, I vow to begin and end with you.* Today is the day we move forward. Not as individuals, but as a team. Not as independent contractors, but as a collaborative effort. I know that forward movement is hard some days, but trust me—your marriage will work if you keep moving forward. Don't stay stuck in the past. If you have a new day to get things right, then make a decision to move forward. Most marriages would have succeeded if they didn't stay stuck in a season they couldn't change.

Tam and I have made a lot of mistakes, but my decision to move forward is proven in my commitment to let things go. What has happened has happened. The past cannot be changed, altered, or amended. In order to get better, I've got to move forward!

Till death do us part—As long as I'm breathing, I vow to love my wife to the best of my ability. As long as there is breath in my body, I will do my best to honor my wife as my pride and joy.

Our wedding vows are everything to us. They're like our mission statement, reminding us of our shared vision, purpose, and objectives. Our vows remind us of what matters. Our vows are a living document that helps us to evaluate the success or failure of our current season. When temporary distractions try to move us in the opposite direction, we turn to our vows to remind us of who we are and what we committed to. Everybody needs something to remind them of who they are. For Christians, our Bibles do the same thing. When we read Scripture, it strengthens us for the journey. It helps us to make the right decisions. It keeps us in alignment when we veer off.

Everyone will make mistakes. No one is perfect. We say all the time that neither of us is perfect, but we are perfect for each other. God made us for each other. Tam is my rib. I am her Adam. Tam is my treasure. I am her treasure chest. (You see what I just did right there?) We are committed to one another . . . till death do us part.

COMMITTED TO ONE ANOTHER

Commitment to one another doesn't mean you have to do everything together. Nor does it mean you can't have a life of your own. David and I enjoy doing life together, but his hobbies are not my hobbies. What gives him joy is not always what gives me joy. I like to get my hair done. I like to go shopping. I like to hang out with my girlfriends from time to time and talk about girly things. David enjoys being outside. He enjoys working on things until he's figured them out. David can stay up all night until he's figured out how to work a gadget. I don't have the patience for that, but that gives him joy. We both like to sing. We both like to go to church. But we have different passions for different things.

My personal commitment to enjoy what I enjoy never trumps my commitment to honor and love my spouse. There is so much power in honoring your commitment, keeping your promises, and remaining true to your word. The more faithful you are to keeping your promises, the more secure your spouse will be.

I know marriage has its challenges, but I am committed to never let the challenges drown out the joy. It's a good thing to be married. It feels so good to know that I don't have to make every decision on my own. It feels good to have a partner for life, someone who is always in my corner. Because of David's commitment to me, I get support, strength, encouragement, and love. And because of my commitment to him, he gets prayer, wisdom, affirmation, and someone beautiful on his shoulder to take pictures with.

PRIORITIES

Like David said, our marriage is our priority. We are committed to that. So many people have their priorities in the wrong place. They put work over their spouse, or church over their family, and God is a God who does things for a reason. When he created the world, he made the trees, the water, the light and the darkness, and living creatures before he made us. The order was important. If he had made us before he made the plants and animals, we would have had nothing to eat. We would have starved to death. In the same way I believe that when you commit to making your marriage the first thing on the list that requires your attention and investment, it will help put everything else in its proper place.

I made a decision a long time ago that I would always love David. If he gained weight or lost it, I would always love him. If he was having a good day or a bad day, I made a commitment to always love him. Our commitments are made when times are good, but our commitments are proven when times are bad. No matter what life brings, I cling to David's promise: "It's us against the world." When he spoke those words to me in the beginning of our marriage, the walls in my heart began to come down. I believed him. I knew that God would work it out.

> I cling to David's promise: "It's us against the world." When he spoke those words to me in the beginning of our marriage, the walls in my heart began to come down.

When you honor your commitment to your marriage, God is pleased, and blessings will soon follow. Our pastor always reminds us that before there was a church, there was family. God honors marriage. Before there were children, there was marriage. God honors marriage. Think about the first couple in the Bible: Adam and Eve. Even though Adam messed up, and even though Eve didn't do everything right, they both were able to go through every season of life together. When God sent them out of the garden, they left together. When God created Eve for Adam, he made her so that they could enjoy life together.

Life without love is meaningless. Marriage without joy is a bad business deal. Through sickness and health, Adam and Eve were together. When they had their first two children, they stuck by each other together. When one child murdered the other, they were with each other together. There's nothing greater than your husband wiping your tears when someone you loved has died. There's nothing more comforting than a wife who knows just what to say when you are battling insecurity. God made you as a perfect match for your mate. Everything won't be perfect all the time, but he is perfect for you, and you are perfect for him.

MAINTENANCE PLAN

Every once in a while, David and I will review our vows and revisit our commitments. Life has taught us that commitments are important, but revisiting those commitments is even more important. It's like buying a car. When you get that fresh new car, it's beautiful. You can't wait to drive it off the lot. But if you never maintain it after it leaves the lot, you will do more damage than good.

In the same way marriage needs maintenance. Some people think they need a new spouse when what they really need is a better maintenance plan. No matter how great the vehicle, every car runs out of gas if there is no new fuel put in. Every car needs an oil change, brakes, and tires—and the frequency of the check-ups depend on how often you drive it.

The more David and I have going on in our lives, the more we have to check in with each other. When I'm feeling out of sorts, I have to sit down and ask myself: *Do I still like him? Am I overworked? Am I projecting my pain onto him? Am I nervous about aging with him? Am I overwhelmed and it's seeping into our relationship? Does he satisfy me still? Do I still enjoy being around him? Have I lost touch of what he needs in order to be satisfied?*

These minor maintenance check-ins—done individually and together—have helped our vehicle of love keep running well for more than thirty years. It didn't happen simply because we fell in love. No, even during the "check engine light" seasons, we reminded ourselves of our commitment. We promised that we would fight for each other. Through the rough times and through the joyful times—either way we were going to do it together.

Trust me, God can bring new love into an old marriage. God can restore what's been broken. I'm a living witness that if two people make a decision to work together through it all, God will help you survive every season.

SEASONS OF LOVE

As it is with life, it is with love. Every marriage has seasons. You will experience the summer of passion in cycles and stages of your marriage. During that season you can't keep your hands off of each other. It seems like when you see them, you are immediately drawn to them as if it were the first time. Cherish the summer days so you'll remember them when winter comes. Cherish the days when you can hold her hand on the beach, because there may come a day when you will have to push her in a wheelchair. There may come a day when it will be hard to come home at night because of the stress you feel outside your door. The summer season helps you push through it.

You will have fall seasons as well. That's when things begin to shift very quickly and what once provided shade and shelter is now withering away like the wind. In the fall you've got to learn how to change clothes, metaphorically speaking. In the fall season, you learn to value the layers of love. You learn to see your spouse for all the things they do to cover, protect, keep, and nourish you. You learn to appreciate all the things that make your spouse beautiful, even when certain things change. Like valuable wine, your spouse will age with grace.

When the winter comes, you learn how to hold each other close. When parents pass away and when sudden loss comes, it's your spouse who will bring you the news or hold you while you are grieving. In the winter seasons it will feel cold some nights. You may even wonder if you made the right choice. But don't let the season last longer than it should. For every winter there is a comforter. Find a comforter to wrap your marriage in. Find a counselor to talk you through the chilling winter nights. Find a book to read or a movie to watch to help you endure the blizzards that happen to every marriage at some point in time. This is what life is about.

When you are committed to loving each other in every season, moments will turn into memories. When you are committed, you will find the good in every situation. You will discover that it doesn't take a lot of money to have a good time; it just takes two people who want to be around each other. In the winter you learn to keep the main thing . . . the main thing. You learn to value the invaluable qualities in each other. You learn to cuddle more, argue less, and pray together.

Then comes spring. Spring reminds you that seeds buried alive never die. Spring reminds you that there is always a brighter day. Spring assures you that it won't be like this always. Spring is a time for fresh perspective, new growth, and beautiful love.

The more I get to know Tam, the more I fall in love with her. Having shared my life with her for more than three decades, I have seen her in every season, and yet I find new things to love about her every day. These seasons strengthen me. They secure me. And now I can say with certainty that I am committed to every season of my marriage.

I am committed to loving him through his worrisome winters.

I am committed to loving her during her hot-flash summers.

I am committed to loving him even if he experiences failure in the fall.

And I am committed to wiping her tears during the sad, rainy days of spring.

The seasons have given us a new reason to honor our commitment.

WILL YOU PRAY WITH US?

Heavenly Father,
Help us stay committed to our marriage through every sea-son of life. Through the good and the bad, help us to prioritize each other. Grant us the grace to endure the difficult seasons,

and give us the peace that surpasses understanding. Remind us of our vows when our faith gets tired. We trust you to be the glue that holds us together. In Jesus' name, amen.

DISCUSSION QUESTIONS

1. What commitments have you made in your marriage? What promises do you struggle to keep when the going gets tough?
2. Do you still have a copy of your wedding vows? If so, when is the last time you've read them together?
3. If you have your vows, revisit your commitments. After reading them, is there anything in your vows that has inspired you to live and love your spouse differently?
4. If you never exchanged vows, or if you have no record of them, rewrite new vows today. Share them with your spouse, and outline your new levels of commitment to one another.
5. Think about a time when your spouse's commitment to you became definite and sure. If your spouse is inclined to do so, share stories with one another.

CHAPTER 10

BLENDED AND BLESSED

What Family Looks Like for Us

Family is family, whether it's the one you start out with, the
one you end up with, or the family you gain along the way.
—GLORIA PRITCHETT

F amily is everything to Tam and me. It is our motivation. It is our
refuel zone. It is our war zone. It is the place where our greatest memories exist. It is the place of our greatest joy and our deepest
pain. Our family is the most important ministry we have been given,
and as such, we have learned many life lessons from it.

We always like to say our family is blended and blessed.

The term *blended family* is thrown around a lot these days. The
truth is every family is blended. Two people from different families
fall in love and form a new family one way or another. Some of us are
just more blended than others. Tam and I first committed to each
other; then we tried to create a loving environment where our kids

could feel safe and loved and where they could learn and grow—until the time came for them to go blend somewhere else. It's not much more complicated than that.

BLENDING IN

You learn a lot about your values as a couple when you meet challenges together. For example, when we found out I had a daughter from a previous relationship, Tam and I had been married just a few years. Tiffany was five when we met her for the first time. She had a beautiful smile and a vibrant personality. She was a precocious kid with many gifts. She could sing. She could dance. She could act. You name it, she did it. The moment I laid eyes on her, I knew she was my daughter. And when Tam met her, she embraced Tiffany as her own.

We wanted to introduce her to her brother and sisters, but in order to do so, Tam and I needed to set up some rules of engagement. Our primary rule was simple: every child in this family shall be loved equally and embraced fully. That meant every child would be praised for their strengths. Every child would be corrected when they misbehaved. Every child would be celebrated when they excelled. Every child would be challenged to be and do their best. Tiffany would be no different.

I wanted to give Tiffany the love that she deserved because the truth is, she didn't ask to be put in this position. She was innocent. She was beautiful. She was funny too! And I was clear about my role in her life. I never tried to replace her mom. I just wanted to support her. I used to tell Tiffany all of the time, "Your mother is Mom. I am Momma." Tiffany wasn't a stepchild. She was our child. Being that I was raised as a stepchild, I know how it feels to be treated as someone's stepchild. So I decided that I would never put my children in those same shoes that I stood in during my own childhood. Over time my actions showed this, so my children knew what to expect from me as a mother. They knew I would love them all fully in the nurturing way that a mother should—whether birthed from my womb or not.

NO *STEP* HERE

In our home, we never used the word *step* to describe our relationship with any of our children. I made that decision one day after I introduced Porcia to someone as my stepdaughter. It wasn't like me to use that word, but I said it, and I didn't think much of it. But when we got alone, Porcia asked me never to call her a stepdaughter again. She was hurt by what I said, and from that point on I never referred to any of my children as *step* again.

In my opinion, *step* is not just a word—it's a posture of thought. It represents how someone on the outside is seen by those on the inside. It could also represent how that person feels within the family. I know this term works for many families, and that's fine, but when I was called someone's stepdaughter, I hated it. There is nothing warm or connected about that word in the context of family. To me, the word creates a separation between you and your relative.

Tam was adamant about this rule! She wanted to love every child in our super-blended family to the best of her ability. We both wanted to create a loving bond with our children and have healthy relationships with our children's other parents. We determined that with hard work and communication, anything was possible. And it's true. Over these last thirty years, I've witnessed the temperature change in our home from cold to warm as we embraced each child for who they are and by helping them to see they are equally loved and equally cared for.

Not all of our children lived with us 24/7, so that presented its own unique challenges. Sometimes it felt like we were meeting our children for the first time each week when they came back home. But we realized very quickly that every family manages their home differently. Porcia and Tiffany did not live with us all the time. They had two different homes to manage, and because they were children, we tried our best to instill as much love in them as possible.

ONE-ON-ONE RELATIONSHIPS

Love works every time. I didn't have a manual on how to parent our children; I just tried to love them the best I knew how. I didn't want to isolate any child as "special" or "different" because I know what it's like to feel like the kid that nobody understands. I also learned to get to know each child individually. Each child that David and I have is unique. I learned their personalities, their triggers, their favorite foods, their hobbies, and their likes and dislikes. I was determined to parent them well, and I knew that what worked for one child didn't necessarily work for another child.

When the girls were really young, we traveled a lot, so when I came home, I tried to spend as much one-on-one time with them as possible. One day Tiffany and I were leaving an event. As we were leaving, we stepped into an elevator and another lady stepped into the elevator with us. She saw us interacting, and she said, "Your daughter looks just like you." Tiffany looked at me and I looked at her, and we just chuckled. I am much lighter than Tiffany in complexion, but the lady on the elevator was convinced that she was my biological daughter because she saw a real connection between us. She saw love in our eyes. She saw a bond that couldn't be broken. And that day I learned something powerful about parenting. Being a part of a family is not about one's complexion or appearance—it's about one's connection. Blended or not, people can tell who is a part of your family based on how you relate to one another. •

Tiffany just nodded and said thank you because that's her personality. But if David Jr. and I were on that same elevator, and say, for example, he wasn't my biological son (he is—hallelujah, he is!), I believe he would've yelled out, "Uh-uh, that ain't my momma," because David's personality is different from Tiffany's. I love them both the same, but David is more talkative and outspoken (like his dad), and Tiffany is more reserved at times.

To every parent trying to bond with their children, especially as you try to learn to love those who were not born to you biologically, let me encourage you. Blending families is difficult, but not impossible. Proverbs 3:13 says, "Blessed is the one who finds wisdom, and the one who gets understanding." Let us be the first to tell you if you don't already know: it will take much wisdom and understanding to love, live, and find laughter in each day being a part of a blended family. Though we do everything within our power to make our children feel as though they are treated with the same amount of respect, it is foolish to think that all family members will relate to each other like a biological family automatically. David and I had to be intentional. We knew it was going to take work, and it did. As a matter of fact, it took a lot of hard work, and some days we didn't do everything right, but we did it, and looking back, I think we did a pretty good job.

OUR MARRIAGE SETS THE TONE

It always helps when children can see both parents working together, loving each other, and forming new bonds. In our home I picked up very quickly that my children were watching us. As the children saw their parents lead in a way that honored God and honored them, they followed suit.

Tam and I always tried to set the right example in front of our children. From the beginning of our relationship, we set goals and expectations with the family. We didn't argue in front of our kids. We didn't demean their parents in front of them. No matter how upset or frustrated I became, I made sure my kids never heard me talk bad about their mothers. I set the tone in our home to let them know they couldn't come to me and bash their moms. This method helped eliminate a lot of strife that could have easily come up within our blended family. But I taught our children how to handle anger or disagreements the right way, and I wasn't just thinking about their present—I was also thinking about their future.

HANDLING CONFLICT

While David and I are one unit, as husband and wife, there are still certain things that we see differently. Our own needs can weigh on us sometimes, and our own passions can drive our decisions at times. But David and I have learned to stop and talk about it. When those moments happen, we pause and discuss how we should approach each situation involving our children to avoid confusion.

There is no cookie-cutter kid, and there is no cookie-cutter parent. Many times I had to adjust and adapt my reaction or behavior, from kid to kid and from scenario to scenario. I also learned to never tell my kid, "You are just like your dad" or "You are just like your mom." Kids hate that. The goal David set in our home was for us, as parents, to be the example. We refused to bad-mouth another parent, and we always tried to put ourselves in the position of our child. I'd pause and ask myself questions like, *How would it feel to be Porcia or Tiffany? How would it feel to enter one home and hear bad things said about their mom? Then enter another home and hear bad things said about their dad?* I couldn't imagine how conflicted they would feel if we conducted our lives that way. Any loving parent will do everything they can to avoid making their child feel uncomfortable.

Our family is so blended that when folks see us together, the only thing that stands out is the love. Love is what they see first, and love is what everyone should see first in your family.

The Bible talks a lot about love, and parenting is the best way to practice unconditional love. Our family is so blended that when folks see us together, the only thing that stands out is the love. Love is what they see first, and love is what everyone should sce first in your family.

When Sonya moved in with us after her mother passed away, we were a young couple, just married. We had to quickly learn how to parent a teenager. We were determined to learn how to make this work. It took a lot of patience. It took a lot of trial and error. We were *learning* each other as a married couple and learning how to parent at the same time. But as our children grew older, there were times that were more difficult than others. We had to love them through it all. When Sonya turned seventeen, she started running away from our home. She had never really acted out before, but she was finally processing all of her pain, and instead of telling us about it, she started taking it out on us. I had to learn how to love Sonya differently the older she became. What worked when she was fourteen was not going to work when she was seventeen.

CO-PARENTING

When people ask us, "How do you do it?" we always tell them, "God first!" Then we say, "It works when you work together." David loves for our family to be together as often as possible, so the kids are mostly at our house for big holidays and events. While we enjoy this, it is important to remember that there are two sides to each family. It is also important for blended families to learn effective co-parenting. In order for this to work, both parents must be willing to take themselves out of the equation. There is no room for selfishness—that will only hinder any progress that a family can hope to make. But unfortunately, co-parents sometimes mess things up for their children because of past hurt or because of petty feelings. David and I learned to never use the kids as pawns in an unnecessary game. I never wanted our children to be held hostage to my personal preferences or objections. We always tried to take the high road and provide the best tools for our children to live their best lives.

Another important thing in co-parenting is trust. You must try to establish trust and truth with your child's other parent so you can learn to co-parent effectively. When trust is established, confrontation can be avoided. For example, early on we had a situation with a child's birth mother where the child made the birth mother believe that she was being treated unfairly by Tam. Tam did not let that lie go unaddressed. She went to our daughter's biological mother and respectfully shared that she would never mistreat her. That respect and commitment to truth went a long way. As children grow up, they figure out the games they can play against parents who live in separate homes. How you respond will determine how they will treat you later.

Which brings me to another point: everybody must be in one accord with discipline, because kids are very cunning. This may sound funny, but when you hear things like, "She made me clean up while everyone else was sitting and watching TV," that's probably not true. But if both parents are on the same page, then the conflict can be resolved by sitting the child down in front of both parents and seeing how the child will respond. When our children were still young, sometimes they would say anything to have their way, not thinking about the long-term consequences of their actions. As the adults in the situation, Tam and I regularly modeled conflict resolution and forgiveness in front of our kids so that our children could one day learn to do the same. When the issue became more difficult to handle, we'd reach out for help from our pastor or from a trusted friend. We always tried to resolve the issue as quickly as possible. Why? Because unresolved conflict is never the answer. Like the Bible says, "Do not let the sun go down on your anger" (Ephesians 4:26).

EVERY PARENT WAS ONCE A CHILD

As our children have children of their own and come to us for advice, we help them see that we didn't get everything right, and they won't get everything right either. But I always tell our children, "Do the best you can, and leave the rest in God's hands."

Since I grew up in a blended family myself, I know how important it is to think about what you say to your children. You have to think about and talk with your spouse about why you feel so strongly about your opinions sometimes. It is also important to know how other lives have been impacted, for the good and the bad, because of childhood experiences. Every bit of who I am as a parent springs from choices somebody made in the past—maybe mine, maybe not. But I've learned to take everything into consideration and discount nothing so that I can be the best parent that I can be.

Most of all I try to remember to show our kids compassion—even when they do things that I just cannot understand. With my childhood experiences stored in my memory, I am now able to show a special compassion to all our children. As humans, we all tend to repeat behaviors we saw in our homes growing up—even the ones we didn't like. All I can do is strive to be better.

In Christ's strength, you will be able to support your spouse, co-parent successfully with your child's biological parent, and balance out your own personal needs.

God will equip us and continue to fill us with everything necessary for our journey. He is faithful to complete what he began. Every human has a weakness, but in our weakness our strength and help come from Jesus Christ. Christ's strength is the strength that you are going to need to be an effective member of your blended family. In Christ's strength, you will be able to support your spouse, co-parent successfully with your child's biological parent, and balance out your own personal needs.

TRUST IN GOD

There's a great gospel song that says, "Turn your pressure into praise!" This is exactly what David and I try to do in our family: allow pain to push us into purpose. The reality is, God purposed us to be together and parent these children. As believers, we know God will not call us to do something without equipping us for the journey. We know God will use everything in our pasts for good. Though it may be difficult to see, especially in the midst of life's trials, God will indeed use it all.

Tam and I both grew up trusting God's provision, so this wasn't a stretch for us. But I believe there is a special layer of trust necessary when you have a blended family. In the same way that it takes God being your foundation in order to have a successful marriage, it is also going to take God being your foundation for a successful blended family (or any other type of family, for that matter). As much as we'd like it another way, the truth is there is no shortcut in life. There definitely is no shortcut in working together as parents to rear children into being healthy, loving, God-fearing, optimistic, faithful, smart, intelligent, giving, holy, and successful adults. I wish there were. I would take the shortcut in a heartbeat, and I would also share what I know with you, but it does not work that way.

BE SEAMLESS AS A FAMILY UNIT

Being seamless as a family unit begins with a strong marriage. Tam and I learned that we must be unified if we are going to make it. One way to be seamless is to not make any child feel like they are not a complete part of the family. We mentioned this earlier, and we are saying it again because it is very important. If you are not careful, you can make a child very nervous. After a while, they may feel as if they cannot give their complete heart to their dad or their mom.

Seamless also means no outsider knows *who's who* in our family. It's intentional to our unity that, as we're planning and making decisions, we ask questions like: "Would this be hurtful to either one of us, to our marriage, to our children, or to others?" If the answer is yes, then it's time to regroup and think again. And while being in any family, like a blended family, has its own set of challenges, the rewards are greater than the process it took to get there.

WILL YOU PRAY WITH US?

Father, help us to keep our marriage blessed, happy, and whole according to your divine will. Help us to be the parents our children need in childhood and in adulthood. Give us your grace and strength to get through each day, and show each of our children the amazing love that you have always shown to us. May our lives be an example to others that blended families can work. And whatever our family may be facing, may we always know that we can do this through Christ who gives us strength. In Jesus' name we pray, amen.

DISCUSSION QUESTIONS

1. As you think about the dynamic of your family, what family struggles need to be overcome right now, both collectively and individually?

2. What incremental changes can be made today so that your entire family can become better? (For example, family meetings, counseling, short-term goals, and so on.)

3. If you are a part of a blended family, how might you work to better co-parent with your children's biological parent(s) in the future?

4. When you think about your childhood experiences, has anything from your past affected your present role as a parent?

5. What positive lessons did you learn from your parents? Can you think of any unhealthy patterns that you may have picked up from your parents?

BONUS ACTIVITY: PARENTING STRATEGIES

Whether you have a blended family or another type of family dynamic, it is important that you are intentional about pursuing and acting on strategies to have a more united family. Keeping this in mind, on separate pieces of paper, identify three strategies that can be taken from this chapter. Once determined, come back together and jot your ideas down in the following chart. Then transfer only the strategies on which you both agree to the "Our Strategies" column.

His Strategies	Her Strategies	Our Strategies

His Strategies	Her Strategies	Our Strategies

CHAPTER 11

COMMUNICATION

The Art of Arguing

Say what you mean, but don't say it mean.

—ANDREW WACHTER

It still amazes me whenever I hear people say that our marriage has inspired them. I can't tell you how many times we have been stopped in the airport or interrupted during dinner to receive warm, loving words of gratitude from people we've never met before. It amazes me and it humbles us both because we know the truth. Our marriage isn't perfect, but my wife is perfect for me. Our lives aren't a fairy tale, but despite the obstacles that every marriage will inevitably face, our goal is to live happily ever after. We've always told our children that we are a work in progress. We don't get it right all the time, and most times we learn as we go along, but every day, we try to do the best we can to express unconditional love toward each other.

Some days are easier than others. Even after thirty-plus years of marriage, Tam and I still disagree. I get on her nerves, and she gets on my nerves. Some days she will say something that sends me through the roof. Other days I just don't feel like holding her hand in church.

David, you know that's not true. There isn't a day that goes by that you don't want to hold my hand. And in church you sometimes try to do more than that! Lord, help him, Jesus.

Well, that's true. But I guess what I'm trying to say is that our marriage has only worked because we were committed to work through the difficult moments. We were committed to communicate in a way that honors one another and doesn't diminish each other. But that took time. It took time to shift from arguing to be right into communicating to be understood. But communication has been the binding force of our marriage. When we communicate respectfully, it always improves our intimacy, joy, and connection. But when we press each other's buttons, cut each other off in the middle of a sentence, and raise our voices at each other, it interrupts our marital flow. Trust me. There have been days when our marital flow has been interrupted.

It took time to shift from arguing to be right into communicating to be understood.

Several days, David. Several days.

Okay, Tam, remember the day when you started yelling at the top of your lungs at me about something, and your excuse was that you had to yell because you were a soprano?

Well, in my defense, I am a soprano. So, yes, it may sound like I am yelling, but in actuality I'm just warming up my vocal cords. I am expressing myself at the highest level of my ability.

Okay, I can't even continue with that line of reasoning. David is right. Some days I raised my volume unnecessarily. I equated arguing with yelling because that was the model set before me in my childhood. Like other items of baggage that I brought into my marriage, yelling and cutting someone off was a horrible tendency that I picked up from my family. Whenever someone wanted to communicate, they would yell because they felt they weren't heard. What I know now is that two people yelling are never heard. What I also know is that it is very hard to hear my husband when I am planning what I will say in response to his words while he is still speaking. I have learned to pause, pray, and follow the words of Scripture—be quick to hear, slow to speak (James 1:19). It has not always been easy, but over the years I've gotten better at it.

Tam and I have had our share of arguments in the past. But the one argument that takes the cake is the argument that happened over a tuna fish sandwich. You read that right—over a tuna fish sandwich.

How could I forget that one?

Right. I'll never forget it myself. It was a regular day in the Mann residence. We had only been married for a few years, and Tam was working at Pearle Express. I was doing hair for a living, so our salaries were minimal at the time. We did the best we could with what we had, but we both had to work in order to make ends meet. That particular day Tam had worked an incredibly long shift, and as is the custom in our home, Tam usually prepares dinner every night and I help to clean up after dinner is served. Well, Tam was nowhere to be found, and it was dinnertime. My stomach was singing to the tune of "Oh Happy Day," and I would've made a meal in the meantime to hold me over, but I assumed Tam was coming home immediately after work. It turns out, however, that Tam made a "pit stop" to the grocery store, and a pit stop is never a quick in-and-out undertaking with Tam. If you know anything about my wife, you know that going to the grocery store is a great adventure. Tam typically goes to five stores to get three items! She will buy meat from one place, canned goods from another place, and milk from the store ten miles away.

In my defense, sir, I am trying to be a great steward of our finances. I want to be wise with my spending, so, yes, I will travel to a few places to secure the greatest discount.

The only problem, dear, is that the gas you expend to get to those three stores exceeds the money you would've spent in one store trying to save in another store. You see? We're arguing now . . .

We're not. This is just intense dialogue.

I love you, too, Momma. So, back to my story. When Tam finally got home, it was time for breakfast the next day. No, it wasn't that bad. But I do recall asking her where she had been all day. She told me she made a quick stop to the grocery store, and I didn't bother to follow up with any more questions. I knew what that meant so I left it alone. I also knew that she was about to throw down in the kitchen, so I waited to smell the fresh peppers and onions sizzling over a succulent steak with a side of macaroni and cheese and collard greens. And let's not forget the corn bread. My mouth was watering in anticipation of this amazing five-course meal, but to my surprise Tam walked into the bedroom with a tuna fish sandwich.

"Instead of me cooking a big meal tonight, let's do tuna and chips," Tam murmured.

I reluctantly obliged. I didn't like tuna fish, and I really didn't want to eat a sandwich. But I guess beggars can't be choosers, and if I wanted a five-course meal, I should've had it prepared for Tam when she got home, not the other way around. So I relented. I didn't want to argue, and I was so hungry at this point that tuna would've probably tasted like steak. Everyone in the family kept raving and ranting about Tam's world-famous tuna, so I grabbed the plate, blessed the food, and went in for the kill.

The plate was pretty simple. Tuna and chips. That was it. I bit into the sandwich while Tamela took off her shoes after a long day of working and grocery shopping. I tasted the tuna, and it was good. But something was missing. Before I could collect myself and rearrange my words, I blurted out, "Did you put relish on this sandwich?" I thought it was a simple question to ask. The sandwich was good, but it was missing that extra kick to take it over the top. Mind you, I was grateful for the tuna and for the chips, and for the plate on which it was served, but I wanted some more relish.

Tam turned around and gave me the look of death. Her first sentence started in high soprano, so I knew something was wrong, but I didn't understand what she was saying because she was talking and yelling and screaming so fast in jumbled jargon! What I remember her saying was that she was tired and she took her time to serve me, and I had the nerve to ask for something additional to what she gave when I could've gotten up and walked over to the refrigerator and gotten the relish myself.

She had a valid point. But instead of hearing what she was really trying to say—*David, honey, I feel unappreciated*—I clapped back. "Well, you are tired, but I've been home all day and all night waiting for you to come home! We've got these kids sitting around the house, and you obviously don't care about me or the kids because if you did, you would've at least come home a little earlier, and if you had, then I would've been able to get my relish. I didn't want tuna anyway. You're always giving me something I didn't ask for."

I literally saw the hair on David's head rising. Scratch that. He was bald at that point, so there was no hair to be raised. But I knew our conversation was sizzling past boil. I could've stopped him mid-sentence and said, "Baby, I'm sorry. This is getting out of hand." I could've grabbed his hand and said, "I love you. Let's not do this tonight." There were several things I could've done to stop this argument, but I was already cranky, overwhelmed, and I felt unappreciated for the sacrifices I had made, so I dove headfirst into the deep end of the pool of frustration.

"You don't think I give you what you ask for? What about what you give me? What about how ungrateful you are for the simple things?"

David responded, "Ungrateful! Your mama ungrateful! Your daddy ungrateful! Your whole family is ungrateful!"

An hour later, we had ripped each other to shreds, arguing about stuff that had nothing to do with the tuna sandwich. We brought up unaddressed issues that had been lying dormant in our relationship for years, and we had no referee to stop us. So we kept going. The more I spoke, the higher her soprano became. And the higher her soprano became, the more I spoke. When one volcano erupted, the rest of the lava began to spill out.

Our original argument was about my simple request to have more relish on my tuna sandwich. Tam felt unappreciated. I felt like my request wasn't a big deal. But because we both were tired and irritable, we let a small issue turn into a big issue.

When we argued that night, instead of things getting better, they got worse. What started out as a two-second comment morphed into a two-hour WrestleMania match. After I figured out that Tam wasn't hearing me, I started yelling louder. She got louder than me. Then, when we could get no louder, she jumped up, grabbed her keys, and said, "I'm leaving." Meanwhile the tuna was still on the table. I was still hungry. But now I was hungry and my wife was on her way out the door.

I grabbed her keys in a rush and told her she couldn't leave. But sixty seconds later, I bolted toward my truck, and I told her, "I'm leaving!" *Boy, I was fired up by this point!* I saw the scene in my head, and I was determined to model a good Western film from the American Old West of the nineteenth century. *No guns though. No guns.* I had it all planned out. I was going to grab my keys, slam the door good and hard to make sure something broke on the other side, get into my truck, and hit the gas hard enough that neighbors could hear the gravel underneath my truck. No matter what Tam said or did, I was determined to win this argument. If she called on my way down the road, I would pick up (so she knew it was on purpose), hang up, and change my voice mail to play Aretha Franklin's hit "Respect" every time she called. I was competing for the gold, and I wasn't going home without it.

But of course, the story in your head never happens the way you imagined it in real life. I forgot that my starter was messed up. When I got in the truck, it wouldn't start!

I wanted to laugh at him. He looked so pitiful. In the moment, we were both too angry to laugh, but boy, did we laugh about this later on. When I saw he had car trouble, I took my time and slowly walked toward the truck. I could see him rocking back and forth in the truck—almost like a man rocking his newborn baby—but he was trying to engage the starter. *Poor baby. You have lost this argument, and there is nothing you can do about it.* David was always so competitive, so the fact that the truck wouldn't start only forced him to confront what he was trying to avoid.

As I approached the truck, I could hear clicking noises—*Click. Click. Click.* But the starter wouldn't turn over. I went to offer him my condolences because clearly his truck had died, but the moment I gestured toward him, the truck coughed and the engine revved up, and David began to drive in reverse as I was reaching into the truck to help him out.

It happened so fast. The truck was in reverse. Tam reached in. I pushed my foot off the clutch. The door accidentally bumped Tam on the side. It lightly bumped her, but Tam is dramatic. She flew to the other side of the driveway and looked at me as if I intentionally hit her with the door. But that situation only proved to me that small matters could become major mistakes if I didn't learn how to handle my frustration.

Anyone who knows me knows that I do not condone any level of abuse or violence. Physical harm is never okay, and I have never resorted to a physical altercation with my wife. I really didn't mean for the door to bump her, but it happened in a flash. My Western film idea had failed. My tuna fish sandwich had turned into stone. Tamela was outside about to catch a cold. And I had embarrassed myself. So all I could do was look at her and say, "Did you just make that door hit you? Tam, go in the house right now. I can't believe you!"

I sat in the car for a moment. This argument had gone too far. One small mistake could've injured my wife for a lifetime. Was it worth it?

SOME ARGUMENTS AREN'T WORTH IT

When I think back on that senseless argument between David and me, I can't help but ask myself, *Was it worth it? Did I really need to raise my voice at him? Did he really need to storm out? What was lying beneath the surface of our frustration? What did we ignore that we should've paid attention to?* One argument over a tuna fish sandwich taught us seven lessons that we now consider as we work to practice better communication skills with one another.

1. Stick with the issue.

Whenever I find myself in a heated conversation with David, I try my best to stick to the issue at hand. The issue was about tuna on the surface, but the real reason we were arguing in the first place was because I didn't feel as if David appreciated my sacrifice of love. I didn't feel seen, heard, or valued. I felt, in that moment, that David was being selfish and inconsiderate, and that was the issue. After a hard day at work I needed to feel appreciated. I wanted some affection. I was hoping he would greet me and hug me and ask me how my day was. But David was hungry, and rightfully so. The custom of our home is to eat at a certain time, and I did not call to let him know I was coming home later than expected. I could've easily pulled over, called him, and notified him of my late arrival. He would've then known to fix something to eat to satisfy his hunger, and when I arrived at home, we both would've been able to react to the situation differently. The issues of our argument were about appreciation, consideration, and communication. Anything else was out of bounds.

I, too, take ownership of my inconsideration in that moment, sweetheart. I have always considered myself a very considerate person, and I've tried to display that consideration with Tam in many ways. But that day, I was more concerned about filling my stomach than filling her love tank. From that, I learned to communicate how much I appreciate her sacrifices. I've learned to be more present when she comes home and not flustered or distracted by other things. Now that Tam and I have made a commitment to stick with the issue, our words are no longer weapons. Our words do not break each other down. Instead they build each other up.

When I used this moment as an opportunity to bring up past issues from Tam's family, I didn't realize I was doing it, but I was bruising my spouse with my words. Each time I brought up something that had nothing to do with the situation, I hurt her in ways that could possibly damage her for a lifetime. My lesson was to change the tone of my voice and the topic of my conversation. To never humiliate or embarrass her because she is my prize. To never belittle her because she is my treasure. Instead I need to stick to the issue and ask her how that issue made her feel.

2. Listen to understand. Don't listen to respond.

Husbands, the more we listen with our hearts and not our heads, the more likely we will be to win our spouse over instead of pushing her away. It's taken me some time to figure this out because I am competitive by nature. And sometimes, when I argue with Tam, I still cut her off mid-sentence to finish my point. But that's not a healthy way to argue. When I am aware of this mistake, I try to reroute the conversation as best I can. The goal of any argument is to listen to understand, and not to listen to respond. If Tam is talking to me, I have to discipline myself to let her finish. It's much easier said than done, because in heated discussions we tend to want to be understood first, before we work to understanding. But arguing with your spouse isn't about being right. It's about recognizing where you are wrong.

I could've done so many things differently that night, but now that I have become more attuned to Tam's needs, I see arguments differently. Now I see arguments as a gift. They give me a chance to gain a better understanding of who she is and how she is wired.

I see arguments as a gift. They give me a chance to gain a better understanding of who she is and how she is wired.

I recognize that my words can pierce her heart. My sharp snapback can hurt her feelings. When she shared her family history with me, it made sense. When Tam shuts down, I now understand why. Many well-meaning friends and family members would yell at Tam to communicate their point, and they wouldn't allow her to get a word in edgewise. This rendered Tamela voiceless. How ironic that the one with such a powerful voice became voiceless because of conflict. When I realized that, my commitment to listening changed. I heard what Tam was saying, and I heard what she wasn't saying. Tam isn't the type of woman to ask for attention, but now that I am listening for clues based on what she *isn't* saying, I can give her what she needs without her asking for it.

Arguments allow me to see what frustrates her and what upsets her, and they give me an inside look into her heart. When I listen attentively and purposefully, I learn her triggers, and she learns mine. I learn her limits, and she learns mine. Arguing in a healthy manner helps me love her the way Christ loves me.

3. Take a five-minute time-out when emotions get heated.

When the water starts boiling, I've learned how to back away and take a break. In preschool, they call it "taking a time-out." When a child is misbehaving or a conflict gets to an uncontrollable point, the teacher invites the child to time-out. The goal is to breathe, collect yourself, and then approach the situation differently.

In our marriage I've come to learn how important time-outs are. Some days I just need to go shopping. Some days, David needs to go swimming. After we take time to breathe and think about how we are truly feeling, we can continue with the conversation and grow from the disagreement.

My momma used to say, "It's not always what you say—it's how you say it." When I take a time-out, I can replay the scenario in my mind. I can ask myself what I could've done differently. I can pray for David to better understand how I am feeling. I ask God to give me right words to say so that I am not doing more harm than good.

A time-out from your heated argument is like a commercial break. You know the show is going to come back on, but now you have time to grab a snack and come on back. When we didn't take time-outs in the past, our arguments went on and on. We didn't have a clear perspective about what the other person was feeling. But by removing ourselves from the situation for a moment, we can approach it differently when we reconnect. I've learned that if I continue to yell at David, even if I am right, he is going to shut down.

I've learned that if Tamela is spoken to like a child, belittled, or humiliated in any way, then she is going to shut down. Tam is a yeller. She uses her voice to get her point across, and when she doesn't think she is being heard, she will yell louder. I am a thinker, so I use my mind to argue with words, expressions, and concepts that may feel piercing like a weapon to my wife. The tools God gave us to build us are the weapons we use to destroy us when we don't argue the right way. Tam's voice is her tool. My communication skills are a tool. If I want to be successful in my marriage, I've got to learn to never turn my tool into a weapon.

These are things we now know about each other. But taking a break to breathe has helped us not to major on a minor. Sometimes words get lost in anger. Sometimes our true love can be hidden in hurtful expressions. But I have learned to measure my words with grace.

Did you know it's possible to say the same thing in a different way and get an entirely different response? So, if I say, "You are lazy like your father," that's one way to say it. But what if I say, "Let's exercise together. I want to support your goal of getting back in the gym"?

He's more likely to hear that and feel my love and support.

Couples, whenever you feel the emotions getting hotter and hotter, someone has to be the voice of reason. Healing can't come in a hostile environment. In order to bring healing, you may need to take a time-out.

4. Never make the issue more important than the marriage.

When Tam and I first got married, one decision we both agreed on was that, for us, divorce would not be an option. We committed to staying together through it all and sticking with each other during the difficult moments. We clearly understand that some marriages end in divorce, but we also understand that every disagreement does not have to result in divorce. I never liked the idea of using divorce as an ultimatum during an argument. In my opinion that isn't healthy. Ultimatums produce fear. Ultimatums can compromise your ability to be honest with one another. The argument was about tuna. It wasn't about filing for divorce. But when we make our arguments more important than the marriage, we forget why we got married in the first place.

A bad day doesn't mean a bad marriage.

A bad day doesn't mean a bad marriage. All marriages have bad days. So I've learned to say, "Yes, Tam, this or that bothered me, but I'm not leaving you." "Yes, you hurt my feelings, but we are in this together." "Yes, I may need a minute to get myself together, but I'm not going to allow the Enemy to make you think I don't love you." My marriage is more important than winning an argument, so after we resolve the issue, I work hard to secure my spouse. Why? Because one bad day doesn't have to turn into a bad life.

5. Never retire for the night angry with each other.

The Bible encourages us with these words: "do not sin; do not let the sun go down on your anger" (Ephesians 4:26). That's one of the scriptures that David and I turn to frequently when we are engaged in a heated argument. In every marriage this may mean something different. Some people can't talk when they are fuming. Some people need time to hit the reset button before they try to resolve things peaceably. But David and I have decided that at some point in the conversation, we agree to disagree right now—but we will continue in the morning. I don't want my husband to feel punished for a lifetime simply because we had one disagreement. How often has one negative word or one misunderstood comment ruined an entire day? To me, it's not worth it. I love my husband. And I know he loves me. So I try my best not to go to bed angry at him. Even if I don't want to cuddle and kiss, I can at least say, "Goodnight, Daddy. I love you."

6. Ask for help.

When an issue becomes too difficult for you and your spouse to manage together, then call on an objective third-party member to help you figure things out. Every once in a while, all of us can benefit from a mediator that we trust to step in and provide wise counsel. This ensures that both parties are heard, and a resolve can be achieved. There is nothing wrong with going to a counselor. There is nothing wrong with confiding in your pastor or your spiritual leader. God has anointed individuals to help you to work through your problems when you don't see the light at the end of the tunnel. It is God's will that your marriage prospers, and you must know that God is faithful to send help in the time of need.

Tamela and I have always encouraged our friends and family members to seek counseling. We have often reached out to others that we trust (our pastor and trusted friends) to help us with difficult issues in our own marriage. The key for me was to constantly tell myself, and to communicate to Tam: We can get through this. It's only a rough patch. I'm not going to give up on you, and my desire is to strengthen our marriage by any means necessary.

7. Let it go.

Sometimes the argument is over but the feelings remain. Other times the memory of a harsh word replays in your mind long after the argument has ended. But if you allow your argument to endure for too long, then unforgiveness will ruin your relationship. Tam and I have decided to just L-I-G—let it go. It does not diminish my feelings or hers, but my decision to let it go frees me from my own self-induced prison. I don't know about you, but the last thing I want is to look at my spouse and only see the pain I caused.

And the last thing I want is for you to become the object of my deepest pain.

Forgiveness is not easy, but it is always worth it. Remember, "Be kind and compassionate to one another, forgiving each another, just as in Christ God forgave you" (Ephesians 4:32 NIV). It's impossible to have a successful relationship if you don't forgive. If you're willing to extend the same grace that God has extended to you, your marriage will flourish.

WILL YOU PRAY WITH US?

Dear God,

Thank you for the beauty and blessing of marriage. Thank you for walking with us through the good days and carrying us through the bad days. Help us remember the big picture. Forgive us if we ever used an argument to belittle or humiliate our spouse. Teach us how to be quick to listen and slow to speak.

Help us to learn how to apologize when we're wrong. We will remember that one bad day does not have to turn into a bad life. Strengthen us through hard conversations. Grant us peace during difficult seasons. We trust you to heal every hurting marriage right now. In Jesus' name, amen.

DISCUSSION QUESTIONS

1. When you argue, do you listen to respond?
2. Where do you argue? Have you designated an action plan for having tough conversations?
3. Of the two of you, which spouse has the greatest temper? How can you help each other not to explode during a difficult moment?
4. If a soft answer turns away wrath, how well do you do with speaking softly? What can you do to improve?
5. Do you stick to the issue when you argue, or does the argument open up to other things? How can you rectify that today?

BONUS ACTIVITY: FIVE RULES FOR HOW TO ARGUE PRODUCTIVELY

Come up with five rules to implement whenever you argue. These rules will help to make sure that one bad moment doesn't turn into a miserable life. For example: *When we argue, I will not cut you off while you are speaking.*

CHAPTER 12

CELEBRATE EACH OTHER

Experiencing Joy Together

Every day should be a holiday to celebrate love.
—UNKNOWN

February 12, 2017. That date will forever be etched in my memory. Los Angeles, California. We woke up and realized we were getting ready to attend the 59th Annual Grammy Awards. We had a long day ahead, but an exciting one. Hair. Makeup. Interviews. Red carpet. Sound check. Wardrobe changes. Everything was happening so fast.

Everyone kept asking me, "What are you going to say if you win?" I didn't really know. I had something in mind to say, but I didn't think I would win. Of course I wanted to win, but I just didn't know if it would happen. As a gospel artist in the industry for more than twenty years, I learned a long time ago how unpredictable awards can be. I also learned how to celebrate others. But maybe, just maybe, tonight would be the night to celebrate me.

Finally, the category for gospel performance song was up. The announcer began, "The nominees are: Shirley Caesar and Anthony Hamilton for 'It's Alright, It's Ok.' Jekalyn Carr for 'You're Bigger.' Travis Greene for 'Made a Way.' Tamela Mann and Kirk Franklin for 'God Provides.' Hezekiah Walker for 'Better.'"

The moment was here. I closed my eyes to pray. It didn't matter who won. We all were winners. Travis had been sweeping all of the awards this year. I was so proud of him. He's such a wonderful young man with a beautiful spirit. Jekalyn Carr is something special. Everybody loves Hezekiah Walker. And where would we be without Shirley Caesar blazing the trail for us all?

That's where my mind was when I heard the words, "And the Grammy goes to 'God Provides' by Tamela Mann!"

I was so busy thanking God for everyone else, I barely heard my name. I was seated all the way in the back of the auditorium, so I had to jog to the front to accept my award. I was shocked, overwhelmed, happy, and out of breath! David was supposed to be capturing the moment with his phone, but he was crying so hard you would've thought he had just delivered a baby.

I began my speech at the bottom of the steps. I kept saying, "Thank you, Lord. Thank you, Jesus. Hallelujah."

Everyone was smiling and clapping. I was trying to hold back tears and trying not to fall in my high heels. Eventually I let them go—the tears and the high heels.

I want to give honor to God—Whoo! Thank you, Jesus—it's been a long time coming. OH MY GOD! This is amazing. My mom would be so happy right now. OH MY GOD! I want to thank Tillymann, my team, my glam team—OH MY GOD! My husband—he's the best producer, husband, baby daddy. He's my everything. Thank you so much, Bae. I want to thank my kids. TKO. Everybody that believed in me—Sony Records. Kirk Franklin, my little brother, wrote this for me. I wanted him to come with me. Come on, Kirk! Quit playing . . . we wasting time. Y'all take our picture. My family is going to take our picture. Praise the Lord. Thank y'all so much. God bless you, everybody!

And just like that, I was a Grammy Award–winning gospel artist.

WHEN SHE SHINES

I can't describe how proud I was of my wife in that moment. Seeing her on that stage filled me with joy. I thought about her journey. I thought about the long tours on buses that sometimes broke down. I thought about concerts where the promoters promised to pay and didn't. I thought about sold-out auditoriums where we sang for others and helped them to become great. I thought about movie sets, late-night dinners, swollen knees, swollen ankles, lots of tears, lots of practice, overdubs, background vocals, mixes, mastering, lots of happy moments, and lots of funny moments. When I saw Momma on that stage, I thought about everything and nothing, all at the same time. She had celebrated me in public, and I wanted to celebrate her in private (well, not that way exactly . . . but eventually . . . hey, get your mind out of the gutter!).

After she performed that night and we took what seemed like a million pictures, I thought to myself, *how will we celebrate?* As her husband, I wanted to roll out the red carpet, take her to the most expensive restaurant, shine her name in lights atop a brightly lit bridge, or fly a helicopter over the Pacific Ocean. I wanted to celebrate in the best way I could. But after reading *The Five Love Languages*, I knew the importance of celebrating my wife the way she wanted to be celebrated, and not the way I wanted to celebrate her. So, do you know what we did?

We went to IHOP! Yup. We went to the International House of Pancakes. After the excitement wore off I was hungry, and I didn't feel like all of that fancy stuff. So when David asked me what I wanted, I told him. Pancakes! That's all I wanted, and that's what David gave me. I was happier than a kid on Christmas morning.

Pancakes coming up, my dear! We loaded everybody in the SUV, and when the car-service driver asked, "Where to, sir?" I said, "IHOP."

He looked at me with that weird "are you serious?" kind of face. He knew we were celebrating a Grammy win, so he replied, "IHOP, as in International House of Pancakes?"

I said, "Yes . . . IHOP, please." And he commenced to drive us.

It was a special night, so I let Momma get whatever she wanted. During that time we shared a lot of laughs and joy. Porcia made fun of me for crying the whole night. I couldn't help myself; I was a super-proud husband. I think Tam changed her clothes before we went, but I don't even remember. It was all a blur. Our adrenaline was so high that all we wanted to do was thank God for the win and spend time with each other.

Our celebration that night mirrored our lives. Tam and I have always been simple lovers who were crazy about each other. We've never been too busy to celebrate one another and celebrate our milestones. It is our firm belief that the couple who celebrates together stays together.

THE MORE CELEBRATIONS, THE BETTER

Personally, I've never met a person who didn't want to be celebrated. I've never met a person who didn't like when someone paid attention to their contribution (no matter how big or small). I have heard people say things like, "I don't need acknowledgment or congratulations," but most times, it's because they have been let down or overlooked. So they lower their expectations to avoid being hurt. That's not the way it's supposed to be—especially in your marriage. Marriage is an adventure. Marriage is a never-ending PhD program. You owe it to yourself, every once in a while, to take a break from the hard stuff and celebrate each other.

> You owe it to yourself, every once in a while, to take a break from the hard stuff and celebrate each other.

Every year, I check my calendar to figure out how many ways I can celebrate and honor my wife. I don't need a special day to celebrate her, but I always make sure to do something special for her on her birthday, on Christmas, on Valentine's Day, and on our wedding anniversary. Celebrations are great reminders in marriage. They help Tam and me to center ourselves. Celebrations remind us that the rain won't last forever, and the sun is going to come out tomorrow (thanks, Annie). The gift of celebration is that it forces us to stop from life's routine to smile at one another, commemorate a milestone, or just hang out and laugh.

WHEN IT'S GOOD TO ONE-UP EACH OTHER

In our marriage Tam and I celebrate each other by engaging in healthy competitions. We love to do random acts of kindness for one another so we can one-up each other. If she buys a dozen roses for me, then I will buy twenty dozen roses for her. If she surprises me by having my car washed, I will surprise her and buy her a new car. Okay, that's not true—maybe just get hers detailed and waxed. If she writes me a letter and puts it on my coffee table, I will buy one hundred Post-it Notes and plaster them all around the house with reasons that explain why I love her. The way I see it, it is my responsibility to meet her earthly needs. God supplies her spiritual needs, but God uses me to help meet her earthly needs. At the end of our lives my greatest desire is to hear Tam say, "My husband and I had a good time."

I am just as adamant about doing the same for David. Together, we work hard to celebrate each other as often as possible. I try to make sure that everything David needs and wants is taken care of, and David works to make sure that everything I need and want is taken care of. To me, this is what it means to honor your spouse. Most times couples give what they want to receive. But the key to celebrating your spouse is to give what they want and need, not what you want them to have.

David could've taken me to a fancy restaurant after winning that award, but I'm so glad he listened. He celebrated with me the way I wanted to celebrate. We didn't always know how to do that in the beginning. A lot of times we got it wrong. But now that we've studied one another, I know what David needs before he even asks for it. Sometimes he tells me, but most times I pick up what he wants because I'm paying attention.

If you've been thinking about adding some joy into your marriage by celebrating each other, David and I compiled a list of fifteen things you can do to celebrate your spouse. I encourage you to try them out and see how it changes things.

Fifteen Ways to Celebrate Your Spouse

1. Serve your spouse by preparing their favorite meal.
2. Become their personal assistant for a day.
3. Ask them to hire you as their personal massage therapist.
4. Compliment your spouse often.
5. Figure out one way to make them feel special every week.
6. Write a letter and tell your spouse what you love about them. Then allow your spouse to tell you what they love about you.
7. Make their special day a *big deal* (birthday, Valentine's Day, anniversary). Do it big!
8. Write a personalized letter thanking them for things they do on a regular basis that you may have never acknowledged.
9. Shower them with acts of affection. Give them a real kiss, a strong hug, or a pat on the bottom (a gentle caress).
10. Create a fun scavenger hunt that leads them to you.
11. Appreciate them in public.
12. Cherish them in private.
13. Honor them in front of your children. Respect them in life. Always remember why you married them, and remind them frequently.
14. Send flowers to their job, or hide their favorite candy somewhere on their desk.
15. Send them a "sext" message that lets them know you're thinking of them. Send it during a time when they will most likely blush and least expect it.

CUSTOMIZE THE CELEBRATION

Tam and I prioritize marital celebrations. As Tam said earlier, it's important that you figure out the way your spouse is wired to receive love, and then love them the way they *need* to be loved. What most of us tend to do is love people the way we want to be loved, but that isn't the way God modeled love for us. God could've remained in heaven, but he took on human flesh so he could be our example. God's love through Jesus is a perfect picture of the sacrifice love makes.

If your spouse feels special when you make your affection and attention public, then you should think creatively about how you will honor them. Write a handwritten note and place it in their car before work. Send a beautiful text message affirming them and thanking them for being a wonderful spouse. Use your words to create new ways to tell them how beautiful they are to you.

Normally people who need public declarations of affection are also people who can be easily hurt by what you say or don't say. So if you only claim them in private but don't celebrate them in public, they may become upset, and you may be clueless as to why.

AFFIRMATION

David is like that. He doesn't crave attention, but he loves when I acknowledge him in public. Every time I talk about him, he blushes and turns purple. Dark purple—so dark, you probably can't tell it's purple, but I can tell. David is definitely a person who appreciates big celebrations and public displays of affection. When I affirm him, it helps him to know that I see him and I love him.

You'd be surprised by how many spouses will celebrate everyone else except the one they sleep with at night. Consider how often you smile when your child walks in the room. Does your face light up when your spouse walks in? Do you pause to acknowledge them when you are in a business meeting, or do you just keep on going with business as usual? Those small moments of acknowledgment are so important to the health of your relationship.

I've learned from talking to different couples over the years that everyone wants to be seen and acknowledged. Everyone wants to know that their presence and words matter. Sometimes taking a small second to stop for a moment, look your spouse in the eye, and whisper to them, "Baby, I love you for being you. You're perfect for me." Just those two sentences can change the temperature of your marriage.

Absolutely, Momma. Celebrating one another means that sometimes we have to step outside of our comfort zone. Do yourself a favor and complete this quick activity. Take a second and think of something you can write down for your spouse that will help them to see who they are to you. How are you better because of them? Identify two positive adjectives that describe their greatest personality trait. How have you seen them improve, grow, and enhance your life? Take a minute to write a note of thanks, and place the letter where they will certainly find it. Watch what happens when your spouse *sees* that you *see* them.

> **Watch what happens when your spouse *sees* that you *see* them.**

ACTS OF SERVICE

Now, I may be the kind of person who likes public affection and affirmation. But Tam is the kind of person who likes small gestures of love. These acts of service are little things that I may do to let her know I am thinking of her. If your spouse is like Tam, then you might consider cooking dinner so that your spouse doesn't have to, filling up their tank before work, walking the dog so they can enjoy a nap after church, prepping their meals so they don't have to worry about what they will eat during the week, making a quick phone call to handle some business on their behalf, running a nice hot bath after a long day at work, helping the children with their homework so that they don't have to do it tonight—these are all small acts of love and honor. With every act of service I have learned to think outside the box. It's not always the quantity you spend on what you buy; most times it's about the quality of thought you put into what you did.

My wife loves the memories I create much more than the purchases I make. So I now put more thought into the presentation of my gift than the gift itself. I'm sure you'll agree. It's one thing to buy her some jewelry, but how much more memorable would that moment be if I hid a jewelry box under her pillow? She discovers that box with her initials on it, and inside she reads a note that says, "Reservations at 7:00 p.m." And within the box there is another box, and another box within the box, until the smallest box has a small piece of paper saying, "Look in the refrigerator." She goes downstairs to the refrigerator and opens the door to discover another box within the box that says, "I couldn't afford jewelry for your box, but I have a few coupons to McDonald's. I hope 7:00 still works for you."

If I did that for Tam, she would crack up laughing, and most importantly, she would remember it for a lifetime. She also would take me up on the McDonald's offer, and we would go to the drive-through and use our coupons without shame! This, my friends, is a memorable gift she will never forget. It's not always the quantity; the quality and thoughtfulness count as well. One act of celebration can turn a broken heart into a healed one. One act of honor can build stock in the bank of her soul.

Well, my Lord! Now I need that coupon to get me a vanilla milkshake, David! I am smiling just thinking about how creative and how loving David has always been. There are so many ways to love on him, but because I know him, I also know not to throw something together at the last minute. David is a planner. He makes a lot of decisions in a day, so if I'm going to get his un-divided attention, then I need to let him know what my plans are before he gets too busy.

Your spouse may need something totally different to feel cel-ebrated. Your spouse may not need gifts, words, or deeds. They may just want quality time with you. They may want to hold hands and walk in the park after work. They may want to ride down to the beach and stare in your eyes. Usually people who want this kind of attention would much rather save money and watch Netflix at home with you than spend thousands of dollars seeing sites and landmarks that they will soon forget.

Tam likes to do stuff like that—walking in the park, staring into my eyes, Netflixing and chilling. If your spouse is like my spouse, then that means you have to create new ways to reenvision what qual-ity looks like in this stage of your life.

Tam and I are really busy. One month we may be recording a tele-vision show. The next month we're on the road or preparing for award shows. The next month we are gearing up for the reality show. The next month we are scheduling photo shoots for press, marketing, and magazine companies. Our lives are always on the go, and because we do everything together, it's easy to take our quality time for granted. But this past summer we pressed pause on everything, and we went away for a few days just so we could spend some time together. We had fun, just me and her, enjoying the nice weather, food, and entertainment. Those moments are refreshing because they remind us of what really matters.

We started out together with very little, and now that we have a little more, we don't want the more to get in the way of the core. She is my core. She is my world. She is the reason that all of this other stuff happens. It wouldn't be fun if I couldn't turn over and hear her snoring loudly in my ear. It wouldn't be fun if I couldn't share these milestones with someone who has been with me from the very beginning. The stuff only matters when the people who share life with you are there to enjoy it.

SHOW THEM YOU *VALUE* THEM

Every marriage has highs and lows, ups and downs, good days and bad days. If two people want to work through it, they can make it through anything. If you are willing to adjust how you celebrate each other, and if you are willing to do the work that is necessary for growth, then there is nothing too hard for God.

Tam and I have counseled marriages that were on the verge of complete failure. We've seen God restore families after infidelity. We've seen God restore marriages after the loss of a child. We've seen God heal people who are depressed, overwhelmed, stressed, anxious, overworked, and unhappy. Very often (not always but often) the key factor that is missing in the marriage is value. When a spouse doesn't feel valued, seen, significant, honored, and important, they tend to search for value in other things and in other people. We tend to look for others to do for us what God created our spouses to do. If you desire to change the direction of your marriage, do the work. Make a list of your needs as a couple. Ask your spouse, "How am I doing as it relates to loving and honoring you?" Also ask them, "How can I love you better?" From there work on loving each other to the best of your ability, and don't forget to outdo each other.

WILL YOU PRAY WITH US?

Gracious God, thank you for the gift of marriage. Thank you for the priceless gift that my spouse is to me and to others. Help me to celebrate my spouse more this year than I have in past years. Help us not to focus so much on what is going wrong that we forget to celebrate what is going right. May our love deepen more and more as the years go by. We trust that you will keep us focused on you and focused on each other. In Jesus' name, amen.

DISCUSSION QUESTIONS

Fill out the following questions with your spouse. Knowing the answers to each question will help you to celebrate your spouse with more specificity and intentionality. After you've written down your answers, see if your spouse can guess the answers you wrote without looking at your responses.

1. What is your favorite color?
2. What is your favorite movie?
3. What is your favorite season of the year?
4. What did your spouse get you for Christmas last year?
5. What do you love to do that doesn't cost any money?
6. Where can you go outdoors to be renewed?
7. What is something you've never done but you want to do?
8. Do you have a bucket list? What's on it?
9. What did you like to do when you first started dating that you no longer do as a married couple?
10. Where is an exotic place you'd like to visit within the next three years?

BONUS ACTIVITY: THIRTY DAYS OF CELEBRATION CHALLENGE

In the following chart, create thirty ways to celebrate your spouse for thirty days. Each day should be different from the day before. You can do a different deed every day for thirty days, or you can select thirty random days in the year. Either way, think outside the box. Think about their hobbies, their favorite movies, their favorite foods, and so on. Think about what helps them to relax and what allows them to feel loved. Think about their love language and their favorite space to be. Remember: celebrations don't have to cost money or even take them out of their routine. Craft a plan to celebrate your spouse for thirty days, and then do it when they least expect it!

Day 1
Day 2
Day 3
Day 4
Day 5
Day 6
Day 7
Day 8
Day 9
Day 10
Day 11
Day 12
Day 13
Day 14
Day 15
Day 16
Day 17
Day 18
Day 19
Day 20

Day 21
Day 22
Day 23
Day 24
Day 25
Day 26
Day 27
Day 28
Day 29
Day 30

CHAPTER 13

COMPASSION

Love for a Lifetime

Marriage is a thousand little things. It's giving up your right to be right in the heat of an argument. It's forgiving another when he lets you down. It's loving someone enough to step down so he can shine. It's friendship. It's being a cheerleader and a trusted confidante. . . . It's grace.

—DARLENE SCHACHT

In a recent interview a question was asked to both David and me: "If you knew you'd only have one final conversation with your spouse, what would you tell them?" Immediately, three words came to mind: *I love you.* The last thing I would say to David is something I say to him all the time. I love you.

I honestly can't imagine life without David. I can't imagine doing life with any other person. David is my friend and my lover. He's my baby daddy, he's my strong tower, and really he's my everything. He is my Superman. I know he has faults, and I know he can mess up just like I can. But the very thought of living without him is a sobering reminder of my love for him.

When the interviewer asked, "David, what about you?" I couldn't answer without tearing up. I know it's inevitable—one day we will wake up and one of us will not be here, but life doesn't make sense without Tam. I love her with every part of me. Our passion and love for each other is unmatched. I love her with my soul. I love her with every fiber of my being. Above the million things I would say and could say, I would want her to know that I love her. There is no possible way that anyone else could enhance my life the way she has. She may try, but she could never love me as much as I love her. That's the truth. I know this because many times my love for Tam was tested. And love isn't love unless it's tested.

OUR NEW BABY

We were twenty-two-year-old newlyweds when Tam was pregnant with David Jr. Every day was a new adventure. Tam woke up one morning and jumped out of bed in a panic. I felt something wet next to me, but I didn't know how to ask her what it was I was feeling in the bed. There were only two options: either she had just wet the bed or her water just broke.

We didn't think she was in labor because it was too early. But when we got up, we discovered that something else was going on. Fluids were leaking out slowly, and we didn't know what to do from home. So we called our friend Darrell to see if he would drive us to the hospital. We didn't have a car, and we knew that once we got to the hospital we would probably have to stay. Darrell agreed to not only take us but to stay at the hospital in case I needed a ride somewhere.

Tam wanted to make sure there were enough groceries in the house for me in case she had an extended stay in the hospital, so we made a pit stop to the supermarket. The leaking was sporadic at this point, so Tam quickly grabbed a few things from the store to make sure everything in the house was covered. I guess she thought she would be able to shop without interruption. But right before she got to the counter to pay for the groceries, she yelled, "Darrell, I'm starting to leak again. Hurry up!" We rushed to pay for the food, hopped in the car, and off we went to the hospital.

When we arrived, I was a nervous wreck. When the nurse asked me to provide preliminary information for my wife, I couldn't even remember our address! I couldn't remember her birthday. I knew she was born in June, but I couldn't remember anything else. Finally the nurse looked at me and said, "Sir, we'll just get the information later."

They moved Tam into a room. I was so nervous. I was walking back and forth, pacing and trying to calm down. Then a nurse walked in to examine how far Tam had dilated. He happened to be a male nurse, and I'll never forget him because when he saw me in the delivery room, he looked at Tam and then looked at me.

"Can I help you, sir?" I asked kindly.

"Yes, sir. You can. We actually need you to exit for just a moment so we can examine the patient."

I looked at him with the most bewildered look on my face.

"You need *me* to exit? Why? I'm the reason she's in this situation in the first place. Trust me, everything you're about to see, I've already seen."

I figured I had given him a piece of my mind. But he still asked me to leave. They reassured me that they would come and get me when it was time. Two minutes later I was knocking on the door asking, "Are you ready yet?"

"No, Mr. Mann, we will call you when we're ready."

Two more minutes would go by. "Excuse me, are you ready?"

"Sir, don't come back," they said. Then they shut the door.

This was a life-or-death situation. I don't think David realized that. When the placenta bag burst, doctors were afraid the fluids would escape out of my body too quickly. They also had to monitor me for potential infection. Because they were nervous that the bacteria might get to the baby, they decided to induce my labor, and as a result, I had to have an emergency C-section. The emergency C-section made David nervous, but he couldn't possibly have been more nervous than me!

While they were working on Tam, I had to figure out something to calm my nerves. I went to the lobby and found the gift shop. They had these blue bubble-gum cigars to celebrate the birth of a healthy baby boy. At that time we didn't have a sonogram to tell us what we were having, but I was positive we were having a boy. I just knew it. So I purchased as many of the bubble-gum cigars as I could afford and began giving them out to random people in the waiting room. After what seemed like an eternity the doctors came out of the operating room and announced, "It's a boy!" Of course it was a boy. I knew it! But I was still excited and anxious to see my son for the first time.

When I entered the room, Tam was still in and out. She was conscious but exhausted. "Are you okay?" I asked. She mumbled yes, and then they escorted me to the nursery where all the babies were resting and recuperating as well.

When I got to the baby window, I looked all around, and at first,

I couldn't figure out which baby was mine. A Latin guy was standing next to me and gestured toward me and pointed to the babies. He asked, "Which one is yours?" When my eyes landed on David Jr., I knew he was my son, so I pointed in the direction of a light-skinned baby with smooth Dominican-like hair. Because my son was so light, the guy gave me the weirdest look, as if to say, "Are you sure that's your baby?" Then he walked away. I didn't care what he thought of me. I just stood at the window for fifteen minutes looking at our child. *Wow, we have a boy.*

As dramatic as it was, the delivery was just the beginning of our journey. We didn't have a lot of money, so I hadn't prepared to deliver David Jr. yet. In my mind I had three weeks to buy Pampers and wipes, but David Jr. decided he was coming out early. I was on Medicaid and WIC, so I prayed for God to make a way, and he did. As it turns out, a lot of people who worked at the hospital were also close friends of ours or members of our church. Out of nowhere people started bringing blankets, Pampers, milk, and wipes to us at the hospital. When it was time for us to leave, we had enough supplies to last us for a few months! Indeed that was a miracle. But what wasn't so pleasant was that I ended up staying in the hospital for fifteen days. Can you imagine? We thought we were going home, but because of a bad fever caused by an infection, we ended up staying in the hospital for two weeks.

While there, a friend of mine named Sherry Earl was having a baby also. Sherry had a little girl on the same morning I had our son. Both of us delivered our babies around the same time, and both of us had to stay in the hospital due to complications post-labor. Sherry was sick and I was sick, but we kept each other company during the stay. One day they brought a weird machine into the room to pump Sherry's stomach. After she had her baby, her stomach began to swell as if she was pregnant again. So I prayed for Sherry and watched the doctors work on her. No sooner than I finished my prayer, the nurses checked my vitals and discovered my fever had returned. I would not be able to leave until my fever broke.

Not only did Tam have a high fever, but she was in constant pain from the C-section. She had a large incision and couldn't move without someone assisting her to do everything—and I do mean everything. When she needed to go to the bathroom, I took her. When she needed to clean herself, I bathed her. There were many moments during that fifteen-day hospital experience when I had to remember my vows to love her "in sickness and in health." But what helped me to endure the greatest test of our marriage was my friendship with Tam. My love for her transcended the difficult days. I loved her for real. Of course I was serving her as her husband, but I was able to do it easily because she was my friend. It was quite honestly the grossest thing I had ever done. Often I remind Tam of those two weeks so that if she ever doubted my love, she could remember my sacrifice.

Sherry was in the same room as us, so she saw me loving on my wife to the best of my ability. She heard us tell each other "I love you" every day. Soon after, they moved Sherry from the maternity ward to ICU. We later learned that Sherry had stage 4 cancer.

Sadly, Sherry never left the hospital. We both had babies on the same day. We both got sick around the same time. But when I returned to the hospital to visit Sherry a month or so later, I was informed that Sherry had passed away. That moment taught me how precious life truly is. God certainly didn't have to spare my life, and all I could think about for weeks after Sherry's death was how David would've been able to survive as a single parent without me.

I know for sure I wouldn't have been able to do it because when Tam was in the hospital, she was still in too much pain to nurse David Jr. I learned to give our son a bath. I learned to wash him up. And I also learned to change his diaper.

Now, my first time changing his diaper was an interesting act of love as well. Since both Sherry and Tam were sick, we couldn't enter into the room without changing our clothes and wearing a gown. The first time we had to change our baby without the assistance of a nurse, I had on my gown and went to pick up my son. I was filled with pride and joy. He could do no wrong, and I was just honored to be his dad. I took off his diaper. Immediately, the air hit his bottom, and all of a sudden he pooped all over the gown I was wearing! It was dark black and terrible to look at. I *certainly* was not ready for that.

Suffice it to say the moment of bliss was gone. Reality began to set in. Yup, I would never be able to do this without Tam.

Truly, he loved me through thick and thin. That year David could've won the best dad award because he barely slept. We alternated waking up at night to change, feed, and hold David Jr. He knew I was still recovering, so most nights he would let me sleep, and he would do everything he could to make sure that both Porcia and David were taken care of. If you ask me why I love him, there are too many reasons to count. But when I think on the days when his love was tested, I, too, go back to the night when David thought I had wet the bed—when in reality, I was giving birth to our son.

THREE SIMPLE WORDS OF ASSURANCE

The memories of love are countless at this point, but one of the biggest lessons we've learned as a couple is how to say three simple words to each other as often as possible: *I love you.* You're getting on my nerves, but I love you. You just hurt my feelings, but I love you. I don't think you're hearing me, but I love you. I not only like you—I love you.

Our marriage hasn't been perfect, and many times we have made mistakes along the way, but our love for one another is the glue that holds us together. Our love has been the anchor of our marriage. Our compassion for one another has been the distinguishing factor. It has helped us to endure the hard times and enjoy the good times. I promise that if you can learn to incorporate these words into your marriage regularly, you'll make it through anything.

I know. I know. Easier said than done, right? I know. The words *I love you* have been so overused in today's society, but say them anyway. Too many times when people say *I love you* what they really mean is, *I like some surface, changeable thing about you.* A lot of people think that love is about liking stuff. For example, if someone is attractive and they bring us to the right restaurant on the first date, some women think that is love. But love is what love does. If love doesn't give, it isn't love. If love doesn't sacrifice, it isn't love.

The same is true for men. A lot of us assume if she is pretty enough and cooks the kind of food we like, then that's love. But I've learned that real love has nothing to do with a person's outer shell. Real love has little to do with a perfect body shape and a perfect first date. After all, what most people won't admit is that when you meet them for the first time, very often you are meeting their representative. In the beginning of a relationship we all try to put our best foot forward. When we are first getting to know someone, we try to present the best of who we are. We laugh at every joke, wear the best clothes, and put on the best cologne. We try to be on our best behavior. But eventually who we are will rise to the surface. One day they will see the unfiltered, uncovered, unedited version of us.

> Love has little to do with how I feel in a moment and has everything to do with the promise I made to love her for a lifetime.

When I fell in love with Tam, I fell in love with the real her. I didn't fall in love with the representative. I fell in love with who she is, every day, 24/7. Real love is deep. Real love is strong. Love has little to do with how I feel in a moment and has everything to do with the promise I made to love her for a lifetime.

LOVE FOR A LIFETIME

Marriage is a commitment to love your spouse for a lifetime. There are no vacation days, summers off, weekend visits, or refunds. When I said "I do" to David, I committed to being there for him in every situation and season. Honestly, love doesn't usually show up in those first few weeks or months when everybody is on their best behavior. People talk about love at first sight, but love doesn't come easily or fast. Love is a habit that we learn and grow into. Loving someone is about sacrifice and selflessness. I know it to be the case because I've seen it in my own life. True love will survive the pet peeves that get on your nerves. True love will still be there after hair starts falling out or when the extra weight starts packing on. True love can survive the test of time because it is about seeing, serving, and choosing to uplift your spouse. Real love shines brightest when the lights are off.

A lot of people confuse love with lust these days, and I've never seen a marriage survive on lust alone. The difference between love and lust is that one expires. If you've ever purchased milk from the store, you know the power of an expiration date. When you drink that milk before it expires, it will help you. But if you wait too long and then drink it after its expiration date, it can damage you.

How is it that the same thing that helped you at one time can hurt you at another time? Because milk, like lust, expires. After lust has accomplished its mission, it no longer wants to stay. After lust has done what it came to do, it will leave and look for another person to entertain. But love never leaves, and lust can't stay. Lust rarely sees its wrongdoings, but love always shows up to try again in the morning.

BIBLICAL LOVE

When I think about my love for Tam, the scripture that comes to mind is 1 Corinthians 13:4–7. We use these verses as the litmus test to make sure we are loving one another the way God wants us to love.

> Love is *patient*, love is *kind*. It *does not envy*, it *does not boast*, it *is not proud*. It *does not dishonor others*, it *is not self-seeking*, it *is not easily angered*, it *keeps no record of wrongs*. Love *does not delight in evil but rejoices with the truth*. It *always protects, always trusts, always hopes, always perseveres*. (NIV, emphasis added)

These verses introduce fourteen characteristics of love. When I say, "I love you, Tam," that means I am willing to demonstrate all fourteen of these characteristics to my wife. To me, this is what godly love looks like. Patience is the first attribute of love.

Yes, **patience** is the first way to know that love is present. I'm not as patient as David, but I'm so glad he waits for me. As I said earlier, many people are attracted by instant gratification, but when you are patient, you are willing to wait until your spouse is ready. You won't rush them to become something or someone that they aren't ready to become. You'll wait on the things that take a little more time for them. You won't demand that every-thing be perfect immediately. Love allows me to walk with David as he grows and matures. Love helps David to see in me some-thing worth waiting for. When you really love your spouse, it will help you to see your own shortcomings before you impatiently bring up theirs.

Love is also **kind.** By kind, that means I must speak to Tam in a manner that honors her. I learned a long time ago that a soft answer turns away wrath, so I speak to her the way I want her to speak to me—lovingly, thoughtfully, and softly. The question is, are you kind to your spouse? Would he call you gentle with your words? Would she say that you are a safe place for her? Kindness is a discipline that must be developed within us, every day, on purpose.

Love **does not envy**. To me that means that I should never look at something David has and wish that I had it. Why? Because the two of us are one. If he can manage the money better, I won't envy that—I will celebrate that. If he can articulate his words better than me, I see it like this: every time people compliment him, they are complimenting me, because we are one.

Love **does not boast.** I don't know if you've ever met a man who does this, but I know many people who brag about every little thing they do for their spouse. I bought her those shoes. I cleaned the house for her. But when you love your spouse, I believe you never need to brag about what you do or how you love, because when I love Tam right, she will boast for me, without me. In other words, I don't post every gift I buy her on social media. Tam doesn't throw it in my face if she does something for me. Husbands who love like Jesus don't need a lot of accolades every time they do something nice for their spouse. When you're in love, you do what you do because your heart wants to do it. Love does not boast.

Love **is not proud**. You'd be surprised how many marriages are suffering because one spouse is too prideful to ask the other spouse for help. I ask David for help all the time. When we are recording in the studio, I turn to him and ask him if I did a good job. If I'm trying to pronounce a certain word and I need help, I ask him to teach me how to say the word correctly. I think it's so important to remember that two married people are both a part of a team. God uniquely designed me to accompany David in life's journey because God knew David would need some assistance. But the same is true for me. David helps me to be better, and when he helps me, it's a sign of his love toward me. I don't see pride when David walks in the room. I see a partner. I see a cheerleader. I can be naked and unashamed with him because, flaws and all, I know he loves me. I've also found that the older we get, the easier it is to let go of pride. After a while you just start telling the truth. That's what love does.

Love **does not dishonor others**. Sure, Tam has made me upset before, but when she does, I don't run to her family and friends to tell them every little thing she did that bothered me. Married or not, I don't believe anyone wants to feel dishonored. How much more should a wife feel honored by her husband? I always remind myself that God allowed me and Tam to get married for a reason. God put us together as a reflection of his love. When I honor my wife, it builds a stronger relationship between us, and it pleases God. Whenever I speak at an event, I make sure to introduce my spouse to the group. I would never knowingly embarrass Tam. I honor her. So I always try to make sure that at the end of every day, she knows that I love her, and I want my children to see honor in our marriage as well.

Love is **not self-seeking**. Amen! My job as David's wife is to be considerate of his needs. Sure, I will have needs. But my goal is to spend time meeting his needs and trust that he is doing the same for me. That's the way it's supposed to be. As I am focused on him, David is focused on me. When we go out on dates, I'm not just thinking about what I would enjoy. I'm also thinking about what he would enjoy as well. In your marriage I encourage you to do the same. If both of you are trying to outdo the other with love and kindness, there will always be joy and mutual respect there. Remember, you are one flesh. Love and serve your spouse the same way you would your own needs and desires.

Love is **not easily angered.** As a child, I saw how men mistreated my mother. I saw irritable men take their anger out on her. But that isn't love. Love expresses itself. Now that I'm married, I've learned to say what needs to be said, let go of the anger, and enjoy the day. I've learned not to let one day turn into a bad life. When I am too angry to communicate on my own, I use my lifelines, whether a counselor, a pastor, or a trusted third-party listener. I now know it's important to get to the core of my anger so I am not making my wife uncomfortable.

Here's a tough one! Love **keeps no record of wrongdoing**. Another version of this scripture says, "Love . . . doesn't keep score" (THE MESSAGE). I can't speak for all ladies, but many of us are guilty of tabulating in our heads how many times our husbands said something and didn't keep his word. Sometimes we can even fall into the trap of guilting our husbands for the things we said we forgave them for. But I've learned to stop keeping score. If anything, I would rather keep score of the good things David does instead of rehashing the bad things. The way I see it, God loves us unconditionally, and if God can forget all the wrong we've done to him, surely I can do the same for my husband.

> I would rather keep score of the good things David does instead of rehashing the bad things.

Love **does not delight in evil**, which means love does not look for a payback. Love doesn't hope that something is done wrong so that God can teach them a lesson. Love doesn't pray that they lose their job so that they can spend more time at home with the kids. Love doesn't wish evil on your spouse or anyone else in your family, because, ultimately, love is going to make sacrifices without looking for a return.

Love **always protects**, so anytime my spouse is in harm's way, I vow to cover him. Love **always trusts**—and this is hard, particularly when trust has been broken—but love is willing to rebuild even after the walls have been torn down. Love always believes in the best version of their spouse. Love always encourages their spouse to believe in themselves. Love **always hopes** that tomorrow will be a brighter today, and love **always perseveres**. On the good days and on the bad days, love is there to stay.

Now that you've read from this powerful passage what it means to love, complete the following activity. Think about how well you love your spouse according to the fourteen attributes of love we just discussed. If you do a great job at patience, rate yourself as a 5. If you do a poor job of keeping score, rate yourself a 1. On a scale from 1 to 5 (5 being the highest), evaluate how well you love your spouse. If both of you can complete the activity together, it will make for a great conversation about love. Remember, no judgment . . . only love!

Enter your name in the spaces below.

_____ is patient

_____ is kind

_____ does not envy

_____ does not boast

_____ is not proud

_____ does not dishonor others

_____ is not self-seeking

_____ is not easily angered

_____ keeps no record of wrongs

_____ does not delight in evil

_____ always protects

_____ always trusts

_____ always hopes

_____ always perseveres

Enter your spouse's name in the spaces below.

_____ is patient

_____ is kind

_____ does not envy

_____ does not boast

_____ is not proud

_____ does not dishonor others

_____ is not self-seeking

_____ is not easily angered

_____ keeps no record of wrongs

_____ does not delight in evil

_____ always protects

_____ always trusts

_____ always hopes

_____ always perseveres

WILL YOU PRAY WITH US?

God of love,

Your love is unconditional. Your compassion never fails. Help me love my spouse the way you love me. Help me love with patience, understanding, selflessness, and long-suffering.

Help me support my spouse and affirm my spouse as often as possible. Allow our love tanks to be filled by one another on a consistent basis. Teach us to love one another the way the Scriptures tell us to love. We want to reflect your heart. We want to grow deeper in love with one another. We can't do this without you. In Jesus' name, amen.

DISCUSSION QUESTIONS

1. How often do you tell your spouse, "I love you"? How often does your spouse tell you that they love you?
2. Do you wish your spouse was more expressive with their love? If so, share it with your spouse.
3. Ask your spouse, "Am I loving you the way you need to be loved?" Wait for an honest answer. Take note of what they say and how they feel, and try your best not to invalidate their feelings.
4. What did this exchange teach you about yourself?
5. What did it teach you about your spouse?

CHAPTER 14

COLLABORATION

Working as a Team

*Unity is strength . . . when there is teamwork and
collaboration, wonderful things can be achieved.*

—MATTIE J. T. STEPANEK

Tam and I are a team. For as long as we've been together, she has
encouraged me to do my best, and I have encouraged her to do
her best. In some seasons she has been my coach. In other seasons I
have been hers. But we've always been a team. Long before we needed
to memorize lines together for stage plays and TV shows, we learned
how to collaborate with each other. Long before we planned our first
independent tour by managing the schedules of our entire family
(for several months at a time), we were a team. Collaboration, not
perfection, helped us to accomplish whatever goal we had in mind.
I've always heard it said, "Teamwork makes the dream work," but I

truly learned the meaning behind that motto twenty-six years ago on a rainy night in Arlington, Texas.

WHEN THE RAIN COMES

You see, my mother lived in Arlington. Tam and I lived in Fort Worth. We decided to visit Mom to check on her and to make sure she didn't need anything from the store. We didn't plan on staying very long. But one conversation led to another, and we found ourselves there for hours. As we got up to leave Mom's house, we looked outside and realized it was about to rain. No big deal. It rains all the time in Texas.

The problem for us was that our windshield wipers weren't working. We needed a new wiper motor, and we just didn't have the fifty dollars to get it fixed. So for months we played it safe. We knew not to drive too far away from home, and we watched the weather to make sure we weren't caught outside in the rain.

This time, however, the rain was something we didn't plan for. I remember looking at Tam, thinking, *Should we stay or should we go?* Tam, always the safe and calculated one, said, "Let's stay and wait for the rain to pass." But I thought we would make it home if we hurried out before the rain came down. We were only twenty minutes away from home. What's the worst that could happen?

The moment we got in the car we heard the sound of thunder followed by a torrential downpour. It literally started raining sideways. All I could think was, *What are we going to do?* I didn't want to put Tam in danger. How in the world were we going to get home?

While David was asking questions, my creative juices were flowing! I knew we didn't have the money to get new windshield wipers, and I also knew we had to get home. But I didn't let a million problems keep me from figuring out a solution. I looked at David and said, "Grab the clothes hangers out of the back of the trunk."

"Grab the what?" I murmured. Tam gave me a look that said, "Boy, grab the hangers out of the back and don't ask no questions." So I did what every man in my position would do: I got out of the car and grabbed the hangers from the back of the trunk!

I also got out of the car and grabbed a hanger. I untwisted the metal wire until the hanger became as long as a yardstick. David tied his hanger to the driver's side wiper, and I tied another hanger to the one on the passenger's side. Then he cracked his window and slid his hand outside the car. I let down my window, grabbed the hanger on my side of the car, and we created our own home-made windshield wiper! When David pulled to the left, I pushed to the left. When I pulled to the right, he pushed to the right. Faster and faster, we pushed and pulled to clear the rain from our wind-shield. When we got to a traffic light, we took a break. We didn't need the wipers while we were at a standstill, so we stopped for a moment to catch our breath. When the light changed, we got back to work. By the time we got home, our arms were soaking wet, but we made it! We arrived safely, without an accident or any damage done to our car. Talk about collaboration!

To this day Tam continues to amaze me with her wit and inge-nuity. No matter the obstacle, she figures out how to make it work. That's what marriage is to me. It's having the will to work through anything together. It's not giving up when the rain hits. It's not turn-ing around and forgetting your destination. Marriage is all about pulling to the right and pushing to the left when life gets too hard to see. It's learning to communicate with each other and allowing the other to take the lead sometimes. In short, it's collaboration.

For all these years Tam and I have been putting our minds together and working through life's hurdles and challenges. Rarely do you see one of us without the other. Rarely do we go more than two hours without hearing each other's voice. Our schedules are a bit hectic these days, and sometimes we have to accept different engagements apart from each other, but that is a rare exception to the rule. Most times we travel together, we work together, we decide together, and we prepare together. I have canceled several events to be there for my wife, and she has declined several opportunities to be there for me. Our mind-set is: if we started as a team, then we will finish as a team. *The only way to win is as a team.* I don't make any major decisions without her input, and she doesn't make any major decisions without my input. I trust her perspective and she trusts mine. This kind of collaboration doesn't happen overnight. It grows once you commit to working on the same team.

> That's what marriage is to me. It's having the will to work through anything together.

The light-bulb moment for me was when I began to study the purpose of marriage. When I realized that everything has a purpose (including our marriage), it helped me to see my role as more than her lover and baby daddy—I am called to be her teammate and coworker as well.

"SAY YESSS"

In the beginning, I made a lot of mistakes because I didn't see or understand the purpose of our marriage. To be honest, I knew that getting married was the right thing to do in the sight of God, and I liked her and she liked me. So we jumped the broom (as they say) and figured out a lot of things by trial and error. I didn't know that we were created for one another. I didn't know that God had given us a specific purpose to fulfill in the world as a couple. Purpose wasn't a hot topic in church when I was growing up. All I remember was my granddaddy, Roy Mann Sr., preaching with passion and presence in his voice. When I heard him talk about God, I believed everything he said. I could tell that he didn't just love the Lord with his words. He loved the Lord with his heart.

I vividly remember my granddaddy crying out, "Say yesss" in his traditional Baptist preacher kind of way during the climax moments of his sermon. I was only about seven, and I didn't know what I was saying yes to, but I excitedly yelled, "Yesss" with the rest of the congregation, and I would start crying for no reason at all. Every single time I heard him preach, I did the same thing. When I left from hearing him, I felt energized and excited. I didn't know much as a child, but I did learn to say yes to God no matter how difficult the challenge was.

That word *yes* stayed with me even when I got married because I realized that my marriage required a full yes in order to experience the best. In order for my marriage to work I had to be all in. I had to be willing to say no to my own independent agenda, and I had to learn to say yes to us working together. I had to say yes to communicating better. I had to say yes to working through my anger. I had to say yes to making love to my wife (that wasn't very hard at all), but I also had to say yes to being faithful. A true yes in one area requires a no in another area. If Tam and I decided we would eat healthier foods together, I would have to say yes to more salads and no to fried foods. When Tam and I decided to open up a joint account and spend our money together, I had to say yes to transparent spending and no to secret splurges. My grandfather didn't know it, but his words were seeds planted in the garden of my marriage. Each time he told me to say yes, I believe he was training me for the difficult days ahead. But did I hear a lot about how to be a husband God's way? Absolutely not. And were there seminars on how to sustain a healthy marriage? Absolutely not.

David is right. When I was growing up, we didn't hear a lot about why God created marriage. We just knew that if you had sex, you had to get married because that's what married people do. I always loved going to church as a kid, and my most memorable sermon was preached by my uncle Leon. I remember him telling us from the pulpit, "Don't just be a hearer of the Word, but be a doer of the Word." That sermon stuck with me for life because I didn't want to just listen to good preaching on Sunday; I actually wanted to do exactly what God said. This led me to want to know what God said about marriage. Who in the Bible had a good marriage? Who in the Bible had a bad marriage? How was I supposed to love my husband? How was I supposed to care for my family? The more I learned about how to be a wife, and how to be a helper to my husband, the more I wanted to be a doer of the Word and not just hear it.

PURPOSE

Now that David and I have read several books on marriage and attended several seminars about relationships, I've learned that everything in life has a purpose. All of us have things to offer the world. We have talents and abilities, things we were made to do. And a big part of the purpose is to be who God called us to be. Thank God for pastors like my uncle Robert Sample, Pastor Rick Warren, Dr. Tony Evans, Dr. Myles Munroe, and Darrell Blair, who helped us to realize that life was more than roles and responsibilities—life is about purpose. What that prompted David and me to ask was, if life had purpose, what's the purpose of our marriage?

Tam and I were married for purpose, on purpose. It is not an accident that she has the skills that she has. It is not a coincidence that I can manage our money and she can maintain our home. We were framed for one another. God put us together on purpose. This is what has helped us focus on the team aspect of our marriage.

I now see our marriage as God's way of answering some problem in the world through us. If purpose is the answer to a problem, then our marriage was ordained by God to answer a problem in the world. Over the years we've tried to figure out what God wants us to do together that we couldn't do separately. We always knew our life was about more than singing, entertaining, acting, and making people laugh. All of these are ways to help others see the power of family. That is one of the purposes of our marriage. We believe God joined us together to give hope to marriages again. We believe God allowed us to find one another as kids so that one day people would believe in the power of family again. In a world that is filled with so much fracture and dysfunction, I believe God wants to use our family to show others how possible it is to make it through difficult times if you keep the faith and focus on the love. Thank God we aren't perfect! If we were, no one would see how God could turn a messy situation into a message. We are a blended family and we are a dysfunctional family, but we always tell people that we have learned how to put the *fun* in dysfunction. In other words, we don't look at the negative aspects of our family. Instead we focus on how to make the best out of our situation.

When we started to see the purpose of our marriage, we had a fresh perspective on marriage and an even greater reason to stay together. We have more than passion for each other. We have purpose with each other. I encourage you to think of your marriage as God answering some problem in the world through you. Like anything, marriage takes work. But God has put you two together for a reason. God has given you kids for a reason, or God has allowed you not to have children for a reason.

> **Think of your marriage as God answering some problem in the world through you.**

You both came together at this point in time because there is something that the world needs. The two of you are an answer to someone's prayer. That is the definition of marriage on purpose.

When David and I began to see our union from this perspective, we realized how important marriage really is! When our mentality shifted from task-oriented to team-building, it became a ministry—an opportunity to change the world.

IT'S NOT ABOUT YOU

We love Rick Warren's *The Purpose Driven Life*. He begins with these words: "It's not about you."[1] This is also a perfect sentence for understanding what it means to be married. Marriage is not

---

1. Rick Warren, *The Purpose Driven Life* (Grand Rapids: Zondervan, 2002), 21.

about you. It is about bringing life to others, starting with your spouse. Getting married is like signing up to be in ministry. When David and I volunteer at our local church, they don't see a celebrity couple. They see greeters at the door. They see a brother in Christ willing to bring in boxes from the storage closet. They see a sister in Christ willing to help fry the chicken for the woman who just lost her husband. When we do ministry, we are very aware that it's not about us—it's all about God getting the glory. How much more should we think this way in our marriage? The truth is, God wants to get glory on the public stage and in our private home.

The day I grew up into a husband is when I realized it's not about me anymore. It's about serving my wife and our kids, then others through our marriage. When I started seeing my marriage this way, it allowed me to develop the correct mind-set as opposed to making everything about me.

Encouraging families to stay together has motivated me to be a better example in my marriage. Not only is God using us to help strangers, but God is using David and me to show our children that healthy marriage is possible. It is possible to have healthy disagreements without rushing to the divorce ultimatum. It is possible to commit to a goal and accomplish it together. When it gets hard, we keep working and loving. We keep serving and talking. Our marriage is too important to too many people for us to let it fall apart. Trust me. Our responsibility to our marriage is not to prove a point but to be an example. David and I are as real as it gets, but we both want the same things in life—to give hope to the hopeless, to give life to the lifeless, and to help others to restore their relationship if both parties are willing to try again.

None of this comes without teamwork. Selfishness is natural to all of us, and we only curb it when we have a good reason. Marriage strengthens all our worst qualities (like selfishness, for example). Many of us spend the first quarter of our lives doing what we want, how we want. Singleness develops habits that are hard to break. And it's hard to start thinking like "we" when you've always just been "me." I know David had a hard time loving me in the beginning because all I knew was how to fend for myself. Although I was the youngest of fourteen, most of my siblings were out of the house by the time I was born. So I took care of myself. I washed my own clothes. I bought my own car. I paid my own bills. I came into my marriage thinking more about me than we.

A lot of marriages suffer from the same tendency. Because we have been single for a long time, we come into marriage selfishly. We want to keep our same schedule. We want to continue spending our money the way we used to. We think first about what makes us feel good and what we want out of the relationship. This kind of thinking is part of what makes the beginning of a marriage so difficult. But seeing marriage through the lens of purpose can help. Once I started to accept that my marriage was not about me, it helped me to make better decisions at the consideration of my spouse.

A good marriage doesn't just happen by accident; it happens on purpose. Every single time I talk to Tam, I have to decide to speak lovingly. Every time there is a disagreement, I have to choose to love anyway. Many people get the impression that a good marriage has to be an easy marriage. But that's not true. Nobody's marriage stays together because the people are perfect. Nobody's marriage stays together because they always agree. Marriages that weather the storm do so because they decided, "We started as a team; we are going to end as a team."

WILL YOU PRAY WITH US?

Lord God, you designed our marriage for a purpose. You knew the end of our story before we were born. You created us to be an answer to a problem in the world. Reveal your will for our marriage. Show us the purpose of our union. Anything that may disrupt our peace or compromise our collaboration, please remove it. We desire to please you and want to work together as a team. In Jesus' name, amen.

DISCUSSION QUESTIONS

1. What gifts do you as a married couple bring to the world? What problem does your marriage seek to answer?
2. What ministry do you have together? What passions do you share?
3. Beyond your children, who needs you and your spouse? Who have you inspired in the past? Who reaches out to you for advice?
4. How can you better collaborate with your spouse? How can you work together to bring out the best in each other?

5. Who have been models of healthy marriage for you? How have they impacted your marriage, and what aspects do you see in their marriage that you would like to see better incorporated into your marriage?

CHAPTER 15

MANNS ON A MISSION

Serving Each Other for a Greater Good

*If you come together with a mission, and it's
grounded with love and a sense of community,
you can make the impossible possible.*

—JOHN LEWIS

In the previous chapter, Tam and I talked about how we thrive because we act as a team. What we didn't say is that it is possible to be on the same team but not be playing the same game. Think about it: many people work for the same corporation but don't necessarily work toward the same goal. Just because you're wearing the same jersey as your teammates doesn't mean you're working for the same goal. The same is true in marriage. In order for your marriage to be all that it can be—and should be—you need a willingness to work alongside your spouse and a willingness to work with your spouse. When Tam is onstage, I am her support system. I am her manager. I will bring her water when she's thirsty and give her everything she needs to feel supported.

And when David is meeting with the production team for our shows, I know nothing about lighting. But I will stick around to keep him company until the lighting is just right. I am collaborating with him by being present for him.

The same is true for me. If a mechanic tries to overcharge Tam at the tire shop, I have no problem speaking for her. We're not always doing the same thing, but we're always working toward each other's good—for the good of our marriage. When we are reviewing our yearly calendar and budget, input from both of us is required. Tam is not on the sideline of our decisions; she is helping me to make the decisions. In both instances we are on the same team and we are also on the same page.

After seeing my mom in an unhappy marriage for years, I learned how possible it is to be married to someone who fights against you instead of working with you. My mother collaborated with her husband, but he was not willing to cooperate with her. Her marriage didn't fail because she was unwilling; it failed because she was juggling it all by herself. She was trying to be the disciplinarian and the nurturer. She was trying to be the support system and the peacemaker. In her marriage she was the only one making deposits in the relationship while her husband was constantly making withdrawals from the relationship. It's impossible to be the wife and the husband at the same time. So I understand why some people file for divorce. They are tired of doing it all by themselves. Trust me,

I get it. That's why I say that if there is no cooperation, collaboration is really hard.

MISSION-MINDED

My son and I love to watch football. As an avid Cowboys fan, I know what it's like to win (sorry, had to throw that out there). But I also know what it's like to see the coach giving a play to his quarterback while they are on the sideline, but then, when the quarterback starts the play, he calls an audible and does his own thing. In my opinion marriage will never work if spouses are always calling audibles. The beauty of marriage is accountability and partnership. Cooperation is the highest form of marital partnership. When I cooperate, I am willing to submit to my wife and my wife is willing to submit to me. Quite simply, cooperation cannot happen without submission.

Eek! There goes that word—*submission*. Where I grew up, the preacher would talk about submission, and to me it always sounded like women were only supposed to do what their husbands told them to do. That didn't sound like marriage to me; it sounded like slavery. But when I began to read the Scriptures for myself, and most importantly, when I fell in love with David Mann, submission became an easier concept to understand. See, Ephesians 5:22 says, "Wives, submit to your own husbands, as to the Lord." But one verse above that says, "submitting *to one another* out of reverence for Christ" (v. 21, emphasis added). I now understand that marriage isn't only about wives submitting to husbands. No, marriage is about both husband and wife submitting to each other. The husband provides leadership to his wife the way Christ does to his church, not by domineering but by cherishing.

God gave each of us unique gifts and qualities that are different from each other, but when we submit to each other, we help the world see the love Christ has for his church. As Christians, this helped us to understand our marital responsibilities in relationship to Christ. But I have to admit, it was a little tough for the both of us to submit at first because David was trying to figure out the mission that God had for our family. I was so used to doing everything on my own, and I was trying to figure out what and who I was supposed to be submitting to. But the more God revealed the mission that he wanted for the family, the easier it was for us to submit to one another.

> **The more God revealed the mission that he wanted for the family, the easier it was for us to submit to one another.**

SUB-MISSION: WORKING TOGETHER TOWARD A SHARED VISION

Eventually David figured out what the mission would be for our family, and it made a world of difference. David wanted to help people to find joy and fun again. He wanted to see the family unit strong.

When you break down the word *submission*, it really means to get under (sub) a mission. David's mission for our family made me want to support it and submit to it! I think the reason most women object to words like *submission* is because it is really hard to submit to a man who has no mission. It's hard to cooperate with someone who has no vision, destination, or plan in mind.

Ladies, let's be honest for a moment. Have you ever ridden in the car with a man who didn't know where he was going? I won't say every man struggles with asking for directions, but some are too prideful to ask for directions even though they are lost. That's what happens when husbands try to do life without God. When the husband doesn't know where he is going, the wife becomes frustrated and unsure about where they are going together. But when he submits to God, and when he's clear about where God wants them to go, it's easy to submit to him.

I trust my husband as the head of my household because I know he has a relationship with God. When I hear him talk to me and my family, I hear God speaking through him. When I watch him advise our son on how to be a better husband, I smile at the realization that my husband is actually practicing what he is preaching. It's easy to love your boo when your boo is also in love with your God.

UNITY IN WORKING TOGETHER

And it's easy to love a wife who is in sync with the vision and mission we have set for our family. In our home you will never hear me walking around the house screaming, "I'm the head of this household! I'm the head of this household!" Anyone who is doing that on a regular basis is probably not the head of anything. Instead you'll hear me asking for input. "What do you think, Momma? How do you feel about that, Momma?"

I love that I have a wife who trusts me to make decisions on our behalf, but she also knows what she wants in life. When I met Tam, I knew I had to throw away my ho card for life. I wasn't the perfect little angel (as we discussed in the beginning of the book), but Tam made me pause and ask myself, "Am I ready for a woman like this?" She had standards. She had expectations. She had goals. She had been reared and raised by a phenomenal mother who taught her not to just accept anything. The way she showed up in the room caused me to treat her differently from the very beginning. I knew she was too valuable for me to play with, and that's why we were friends for as long as we were. She made me want to be better. She helped me to deepen my love for Jesus. I believe that's what differentiates a girlfriend from a wife. My girlfriends were good company. But my wife was the perfect woman to be in covenant with.

In Christian circles, the word *covenant* means "a sacred agreement shared by two or more persons." My decision to marry Tam was a sacred agreement to honor her and to submit to her before God and before her family. It was easy to make decisions because she wanted what I wanted and I wanted what she wanted.

That doesn't mean we didn't see things differently sometimes, because we did—and we still do. But over time we learned to make sacrifices for the other person. The goal was always cooperation, not competition.

FITNESS OVERLOAD

Here's an example of what this principle looks like in the Mann household. A year or two ago, I became my wife's fitness coach. We talked about her fitness goals, and once she explained her mission, I got under it and began to work hard to accomplish it! I wanted her to meet every fitness goal she had, and I was willing to make as many sacrifices as necessary. I was willing to change our diet, hire a fitness trainer, wake up early, work out even when we were on the road, buy those tight Speedo pants—whatever I had to do, we were going to do it! I submitted my plan to Tam, and she submitted her plan to me.

We were collaborating, but we weren't cooperating. On my plan I wanted us to work out with weights, bikes, and other exercises. On Tam's plan she wanted to work out in the pool, and she didn't mind light weights, but she wasn't ready for some of the exercises I was trying to convince her to try. Over time I noticed some friction during our workout sessions. Tam was moving a little slower than normal, and it wasn't because she was tired.

I was frustrated; that's what I was! And I didn't know how to tell David that his plan wasn't working.

But one day, I just asked her, "Momma, what can we do to help you meet your goal?"

I politely told him that he was pushing me a little too hard.

I have to admit I did get in my feelings just a bit. But I did understand and I apologized. It wasn't my intention to push her. I just wanted to meet the goals she set for herself. I didn't want Tam to feel like I was a drill sergeant. I wanted her to feel like I was her coach. In order to do so, I had to adjust the plan to make sure my wife was okay with the process. What I learned from that experience is that cooperation can only happen when both parties are willing to compromise and hear one another. What good would it have been for us to meet a goal that ultimately made Tam feel miserable? After I really heard what she was saying, I made the adjustments, and we figured out a rhythm that worked for her.

Above all, I want my wife to know I'm on her team and on her page. For us, everything about submission begins and ends with love. I want to love Tam so well that she wants to live two or three more lives with me. I want my wife to see that she is the prize that makes my world go 'round. My wife is not the icing on the cake; she is the cake, the cake mix, the sugar, the whipped cream, the oven the cake was baked in, and the toppings on the side! She deserves to feel like royalty.

> **My wife is not the icing on the cake; she is the cake, the cake mix, the sugar, the whipped cream, the oven the cake was baked in, and the toppings on the side!**

I am not just submitted to my wife; I am committed to my wife. She is the joy of my life. That means giving her my undivided attention. As busy as our lives can get, sometimes I just put the phones away, tune out the noise of outside distractions, and zone in to her. Tam needs my focus. She need my concentration. So I submit to her by concentrating on her, by cherishing her, and by paying attention to her ups and downs, her temperament, and the tone of her voice. I study Tam like fine art. And at the end of the day I want her to see through my concentration that I want her to win, and I will do whatever it takes to see her flourish.

Husbands, I challenge you to concentrate on your spouse, study her line by line, precept upon precept—take inventory and recognize when there is a deficit. When she's low on joy, as her husband, it's your primary responsibility to fill her up. When she's low on attention, as her husband, it's your responsibility to satisfy her needs. Most importantly, don't submit to her because of what you want in return. Submit to her because that is what she deserves—loving her like Jesus loved you without any guarantee of reciprocity in return. When we finally get to a place where we can collaborate and cooperate with our spouses unconditionally, then we have mastered the art of submission.

COOPERATION ABOUT COMPENSATION

While we're talking about working as a team, we should talk about finances: one of the greatest tests of submission is how a couple cooperates with each other in their finances. Tam and I decided a long time ago to be completely transparent with one another about our finances. And in the beginning of our marriage, that was super easy to do because we didn't have any money problems at all.

What do you mean?

I mean, we didn't have money issues because we didn't have any money! And it's really hard to hide or lie about the three dollars you have in the account when you are broke and struggling to make ends meet.

Well, that's true. When David and I first got married, we earned about $24,000 a year between the two of us. I was working at a nursing home, and David had just graduated from cosmetology school. Notice I said "graduated"—not accumulated money or grossed any cash. He was a graduate with bills and very few clients to help pay those bills.

So you just gonna kick a brotha while he's down, Momma? I mean, I was following my passion and trying to do whatever I could to make it work. My mother taught me that that's what real men do. But during those first ten years of marriage, it was hard stretching our salaries between bills, children, and unexpected expenses. One time, after paying all of our bills, we simply ran out of money. There was five dollars between the two of us, and Tamela was hungry.

Oh, so I was the only one hungry that day? So you were fasting and praying, huh?

Well, no, I wasn't fasting and praying, but I was praying fast! On the one hand, I felt a sense of relief because the household bills were paid. We had enough to put gas in the tank. But we needed to eat. Tam reminded me of the butcher shop near our house that had a small restaurant behind the butcher store. On a daily basis they served fresh-cut meat from the butcher, sandwiches, and a few side dishes. At the time the cost for food and drinks was a lot cheaper than it is today, so we knew we could at least share a meal at this restaurant that day. To our surprise, they offered a special where you could enjoy three chopped beef sandwiches for one dollar. *Music to our ears.* In addition to that, they charged fifty cents for a cup of sweet tea, and fifty cents for a bag of chips. We ordered two teas, three chopped beef sandwiches, and two bags of chips. We were able to pay for the entire meal and have change left over. (Ain't God good?)

I can taste that chopped beef now. It was one of the best meals we've ever had because it reminded us that God will always provide. Sometimes David and I had very little money to split between all of us, but somehow, someway, God was faithful to give us what we needed. As our lives began to change and we began to earn enough money to save a little and splurge a little, David and I sat down and created some money rules to live by. We wanted to protect our family from emotional, spiritual, and financial bankruptcy. And even today, we live by these rules as a collective team.

Rule #1: Thou shalt be honest with thy spouse.

Honesty in our marriage looks like me asking and answering the right questions: Are we in debt? Do we have a savings account? How many student loans do we have? If we had to make a big purchase today, are we financially prepared? Do we have any bills in collections? What is the interest rate on each loan we have? I've learned over time that honest, no-holds-barred conversations can save a marriage from a whole lot of heartache in the long run.

I couldn't agree more, David. In a marriage, two individuals with separate spending habits and separate financial portfolios will become one (more and more each day). My decisions and history impact him. His credit and attitude about money impact me. All of this matters in the relationship. It's only right to be up-front with one another as early as possible. But that same honesty has to continue long after you marry someone. It is so important to keep those lines open at all times. Secrecy with finances always spells disaster.

Rule #2: Identify the money manager.

I believe that it is very important for both the husband and the wife to decide together who will pay the bills and manage the finances. If you know you're a big impulse shopper and you're not great with money, just let the other person handle it. It's all about what is best for your situation, and the only people who will know what system works best for you two is you two. Leave other people's opinions out of your financial life. If you think that one person should do it because of how your parents did it or because of your ideas about what women should do versus what men should do or anything like that, get rid of those thoughts! This is all about who is best equipped to do what. Marriage is about two people becoming a team and the team working together in every area to win. Whoever has a mind for numbers and whoever can balance the checkbook and keep the bills paid, let them do it. There is no shame in knowing and playing to each person's strengths and weaknesses.

Rule #3: Create a budget.

In the Mann household a budget is mandatory. We have budgets for everything. We have budgets for our business endeavors. We have budgets for our vacations. We have budgets for our primary expenses. We have a budget for literally everything.

As a couple, we have a short-term plan and a long-term plan. We also have a weekly, monthly, and yearly budget. David does this much better than me, but he helps me plan what we will spend and prepare for unexpected events. He always tells people that we didn't have money in the beginning of our marriage, so that's why money wasn't an issue for us. But I believe that money wasn't an issue for us because we didn't try to live beyond our means. Even now, God has blessed us in many ways, but we do not live above our means. We have tried to keep this rule in place, even as the checks got bigger. The more we grew together, we realized how important a budget was. Every step of our journey, we have worked at developing contentment and joy with what we have so we don't have to "try and buy it." We remind ourselves all the time that going over budget is not worth the pain it can cause.

Rule #4: Invest as a team.

Tam and I are a team. In every way, it is *us against the world*. We've learned together. We've failed together. And if Tam and I knew back then what we know right now about money, we would've made some different decisions early on. One year, Tam and I were presented with an investment opportunity. We weren't rich, so we thought we couldn't invest. In our minds investment was for wealthy people, but we've come to learn that every little bit counts over time. Our fear and lack of knowledge about investing kept us from doing something early that we could've benefited from right now. Had we invested in the time frame we were offered, we could've paid off our first home with the money from that investment. But we didn't know. Our ignorance hurt us. I was focused on spending my way. She was focused on saving her way. But teams aren't afraid to take risks. Teams aren't afraid to do the research and make a decision that is in the best interest of both parties. As a team, we decided to save as much as we could as often as we could. Think of it this way: When you go up, she goes up. When you're in trouble, he's in trouble. Your marriage should operate that way with everything: it's me and you against the world.

Rule #5: Keep it consistent.

Consistency is so important when it comes to how you deal with money in your relationship. Budgeting is not always fun. Living within your means doesn't always feel good. I mean, let's be real here. There are times when you will want to just blow a few dollars, do some retail therapy, and forget about a budget. That's why it's so important that you motivate each other. It's also important that each person be fair and consistent with it. We know of some couples where there is a kind of dictator relationship, where one person feels like it's okay to buy and spend whatever they "need" to, but when the other person brings home a bag or something, all of a sudden it's "the budget this and the budget that." Selfishness and inconsistency will bring all kinds of issues into your relationship. We have seen it with so many couples, young and old. It's important that the rules apply to everyone and that both people know what the spending rules are. Doing so cuts down on resentment and one person feeling like they're being treated like a child or not cared about.

All of this takes work. But trust me, it can be done. When David and I made a conscious decision to cooperate in the area of our finances, we experienced newfound joy, peace, and intimacy.

COMPETITION

You know, a lot of people ask us how we maintain a healthy marriage in the midst of an industry filled with competition. David's phone rings and people want him. My phone rings and people want me. How do we keep from competing with each other? To me, it's simple. We see our marriage as completing one another, not competing with each other. The higher David goes, the higher we go.

And the higher Tam goes, the higher we go. It never pays to compete with your spouse. It only hurts the marriage and confuses the children. Tam and I always wanted to create an environment of love, honor, and encouragement. When she wins, I want my children to see me yelling and cheering the loudest and longest. When I win, my children certainly hear Tam's high soprano screaming from the sidelines. We all win when the other person succeeds.

Another reason we've never had to struggle with competition in our marriage is because we never asked for the stage in the first place. Don't get me wrong. We are so grateful that God blessed us to travel the world and to minister to others, but the stage wasn't the goal—love was. The money wasn't the goal—the impact was. Long before anybody knew David and Tamela

> **We decided that we would not do it for the income—we would do it for the outcome.**

Mann, we decided that Christ would be glorified above all. We decided that we would not do it for the income—we would do it for the outcome, and that has helped us to establish a mission for our marriage and for our family.

WHAT'S YOUR MISSION FOR YOUR MARRIAGE?

What is your mission for your marriage? If *submission* means to get under a mission, then what is the mission that your spouse can submit to, or get under, in order to bring your family into a fruitful life? Have you ever sat down to write your mission for your marriage? I'm sure you have a mission for life or a five-year plan for your business. You may even have a financial plan or a family plan if you want to expand the family, downsize or upgrade into a new home, or help your children get through school. But every marriage needs a mission. Here are a few examples of possible missions for your family:

1. We will be a loving family who will not raise our voices to get our point across.
2. We will love the Lord, love each other, and not let outsiders distract us from our goals.
3. We will never feel more appreciation outside of this house than we do inside of this house.
4. We will honor one another, listen more than we speak, and commit to family dinner at least once a week.
5. As a family, we will forgive quickly, learn often, pray together, and have fun.

Your mission doesn't have to be a long statement, but every family should have a goal by which they live. Every family should have a standard that they aim to reach toward. No one will get it perfect all the time, but the goal is a marker that helps you to stay focused on one another.

As a married couple, Tam and I have decided that this is our marital mission: *We will love on purpose, and we will lead by example. We will never go to bed without making peace. We will support, cherish, and honor one another even when it's hard, and we will minister to people who may be going through a tough time in their marriage.* For our family mission, *we aim to love God, love each other, and have a lot of fun!*

We both know marriage isn't easy. But we also know that marriage has been one of the greatest gifts that life has ever brought us. Through it all, we can write these words today, confident that every season—even the surprises at the door—were worth it. Every tear was worth it. Every memory was worth it. Every hug has been worth it. Every argument was worth it. If you let him, God will work all things together for your good. If you let him, God can do a miracle in your marriage. If he did it for us, he can do it for you.

WILL YOU PRAY WITH US?

Creator of all things, in the beginning you made the heavens and the earth. You spoke the world into existence, and everything you created had a purpose. As you continue to show us the purpose of our marriage, help us to collaborate and cooperate with each other. Remove any competition between us. Restore our joy and reconnect us to the things that give our marriage meaning. In Jesus' name, amen.

DISCUSSION QUESTIONS

1. Do you have a mission for your marriage? If so, write it below. If not, create one below.
2. What are your thoughts about healthy competition in your marriage? Do you enjoy competing with each other to show love or to give affection? Why or why not?
3. Do you see eye-to-eye on finances and fun? Name a time when you may have felt uneasy about compensation but were hesitant to share it with your spouse.
4. On a scale from 1 to 10, how would you rate your ability to work together with your spouse?

BONUS ACTIVITY: CREATING A MISSION STATEMENT

In the following space, come up with your marital mission and your family mission. Talk about it with your family at the next family meeting, and every once in a while, revisit the mission to see if you are all on the same page *and* on the same team.

_____

_____

_____

_____

CHAPTER 16

FRIENDSHIP

What Keeps Us Together, Especially When It Hurts

I found the one my heart loves.

—SONG OF SOLOMON 3:4 NIV

Tam and I met when we were both nineteen years old. We didn't know much about life when we met one another, but before we were attracted to each other and before we decided to date, we were ride-or-die friends. On any given day we'd spend many hours of the day together. We loved to hang out. We loved to have fun. When we weren't talking, we were singing at the top of our lungs. I loved to hear her voice. Her tone, her effortlessness, and her range always amazed me. I could listen to her sing all day and never get tired of it.

During those friendship years we got a chance to teach each other. There was no pressure to pretend or to act like something we weren't, because, as friends, we just wanted to do life together—no strings attached.

Our friendship has meant everything to me. I still talk to David for hours at a time. He still teaches me things about life that I never knew. We still love to laugh together and share memories together that only friends would enjoy. The Bible says "a friend loves at all times" (Proverbs 17:17). I have loved David and seen David in every phase of life. I loved him when he needed rides to get from work to church when we were teenagers. And I loved him when he had his "little girlfriends" before we got married. If he ever doubted my friendship, all he had to do was think about the first few years that we met and remember all that we went through together as friends.

BEFORE WE COMMITTED

When Tam and I first met, I had a girlfriend or two. It's nothing to brag about, but it's true. Tam quickly became my ride-or-die friend. We were so cool that one time we were invited to attend the same party. It was my birthday and our pastor, Darrell Blair (a good friend of ours growing up), called me and told me to come to the Paynes' house to hang out. The Payne family had several kids our age—all girls. We were always going over to the Paynes' house to hang out. I hadn't planned to stay at the Paynes' house very long—after all, it was my birthday and I planned on going out. But I figured I would stop by for a little while and mingle with the crew. When I pulled up, who was one of the first people I saw at the party? Tam. And who was I walking into the party with? My current girlfriend.

As soon as I opened the door to greet Tam, I heard everyone yell, "Surprise!" I looked around the room and all of my close friends were there—including another one of my girlfriends! So, girlfriend #1 was on my arm, girlfriend #2 was in the crowd, and Tam was there just hanging out. She was really my friend, and she was one of the most honest friends I had at the time. She watched me get busted with two girls at the same party who were dating me, and she laughed at me until both of us couldn't stop laughing. That's how tight our friendship bond was.

You would think I was one of the guys when we were younger because David was always inviting me out with his male friends. He didn't treat me like he treated them, though. He never let them make fun of me or mess with me like they messed with each other. You know, guys can be a little rough in their conduct and a little crass or harsh with their words. But David told his guy friends to be on their best behavior around me. He was thoughtful, considerate, and protective, even as my friend, and I never forgot that about him.

Fast-forward to a few months later. Tam was so much my friend that she stayed at the hospital with me until Porcia was born. We spent twenty-one hours in the hospital waiting room, and do you know what we did the entire time? We laughed and joked all night long! Back in the day, we used to laugh about anything and everything. I was always the jokester. I would mimic things I saw on TV. I would imitate people who walked past us. Anything was liable to become material for my jokes. Meanwhile, Tam would crack up laughing at everything I said. Sometimes Tam would be bent over in tears, laughing so hard. From the start we were always having innocent, life-giving fun.

Tam was the reason I could even have somewhat of a relationship with the mother of my first child. Tam was the "middle woman" between us who made sure I was able to spend time with my daughter.

I told her everything about me way before we started dating. Tam knew when I had a girlfriend. Tam knew if I had a "friend" on the side. Tam listened to me and never judged me, but if I asked her opinion, she would always tell me the truth. Never in a million years did either of us think we would fall in love at the time. Besides, I wasn't the only one who had a few "extracurricular activities" when we met. Tam might try to get on me for my dating history, but what Tam won't tell you is that she was engaged!

David!

Ooooooh, it's getting hot in here!

I can't believe you!

What? Tell the truth and shame the devil! It is what it is. Talk about that, Tam! Since you are exposing me. Why not expose yourself?

Well, David is right. I was engaged before I started dating him. And David knew all about it. We were such friends that I told him I was engaged.

Ummm, not exactly how that happened.

Do you want me to tell the story or no, Bae?

You can tell the story, but just tell the truth.

Okay, well, the truth is there was this guy—who shall remain nameless. He was a really nice guy, and he spent a lot of time getting to know me. The only problem is, he moved to Virginia because he joined the service. I thought he was nice, and we agreed to date.

Were you in love with him?

I liked him a lot.

But were you in love with him?

I mean, he was a great guy, and I'm sure he was in love with me—David, let me finish the story! So the guy asked me to marry him, and I said yes. We had talked about me moving to Virginia, but I don't know if I really took him seriously, because right around the time when the guy and I got serious, David and I started hanging out a lot more. David's friends were my friends and my friends were his friends, so even if we hadn't planned to be together, we would somehow cross paths and end up together. One day, I told David's younger brother, Theland, that the guy asked me to marry him. I think I had picked him up from school that day, the same way I used to pick up David from cosmetology school, and we started talking about new things happening in my life.

"Really?" he said.

"Really," I replied. No sooner than I let the cat out of the bag I knew he would tell David. I didn't exactly say anything to David yet because I didn't know how to bring it up. But before I could figure it out, David approached me and beat me to it.

So this is how I remember it happening. My brother walked up to me one day and said, "You know your girl's about to get married, right?"

I was completely taken aback. "What? She about to what?" I asked him.

He repeated, "She's about to get married. She's engaged."

I don't know what those words did to me, but I knew I couldn't let this woman get away. She and I had liked each other, but we were only focused on the friendship until another man tried to take her away from me. Almost immediately, I changed gears and started coming on strong. I started letting go of the other girls I had been dating on the side, and I decided to make it official with Tam.

David knew I was falling for him, but I didn't know how to tell him either. My commitment was to the guy, but my heart was with David. I was conflicted because David was my friend and the guy was my boyfriend.

When I finally approached her about the engagement, she asked a question that she already knew the answer to: "Who told you?"

"What do you mean who told me?" I replied. I didn't say another word for a solid sixty seconds, and then I said as nonchalantly as possible, "If that's what you want to do, it's up to you." I tried my best to act as if I didn't care, but I was hoping she would profess her undying love for me.

She didn't.

That night, Tam was supposed to sing at an event. We didn't ride together like we usually did, so I didn't know if she had come alone or not. But I did know that she didn't come by the house like she normally would. Plus, I heard through the grapevine that her boyfriend/fiancé had come to town and might be there. And apparently he had been making threats about what he was going to do when he saw me and all of that.

Now, I wasn't always a church boy and I had been known to "lay hands suddenly" on a few people (if you know what I mean). So, once I caught wind of what the guy was talking about doing, I went into boyfriend mode, even though Tam was just my friend. In the meantime, Tam was nowhere to be found. She was inside the church, singing with the chorus. So I got someone to get her attention and asked her if she would come outside. She eased down the aisle to come and see what I wanted. But she didn't know that the guy and I were about to fight. She walked outside and saw what was going on. Then she turned around and went back to the choir stand. I motioned for her to come back out, but she didn't want to have anything to do with it.

I wasn't staying around for that. Back then David was the kind of guy that didn't mind a little physical altercation with another guy. But thank God cooler heads prevailed and no punches were thrown. After that night I still had a major decision to make. So I followed my heart and called off the relationship with the guy and married my best friend. (I know it sounds like a scene from a movie, but it's true.) The rest is history.

All this time we had been playing around, flirting with each other, and hinting at our attraction for one another, but that night I decided it was time to get serious. I had never felt the same way about another woman as I had Tam. I'm certain it was because of our friendship. I took pride in the fact that I knew her better than anyone else. And when we fell in love, got married, and had kids, the first thing I told my kids to do when they were interested in dating someone was begin their relationship as friends.

FRIENDSHIP AS A FOUNDATION FOR LOVE

I learned to pay attention to what someone values in the beginning of a relationship because whatever it is based on, it will thrive on. If the relationship is based on money, then the relationship will be great as long as money is in the bank. But when the money disappears, then the marriage will slowly but surely disintegrate. If the relationship is based on sex, then it will be great as long as the sex is good. But if things change and health declines and life happens, then neither person will have anything to cling to, and both people will have a problem. But if the marriage is based on friendship—real, solid, I-love-you-and-I-like-you friendship—then you'll be able to survive anything. I believe this with every fiber of my being. Your friendship should be the thing your relationship is built on so that you have something solid to fall back on. Because one day your wife will not just need her husband . . . she will need her friend.

If that ain't the truth, I don't know what is. Many days I don't think I would've made it if I only had a husband in David. Some days I needed my friend. I needed my buddy to come close to me, sit with me, and talk me through life's unexpected storms. One season in particular sticks out above the rest.

We were on the set of *Meet the Browns*, and the phone rang. My brother-in-law had passed away, and the news hit me so hard that I didn't know what to do. I was right in the middle of a scene, and one of the assistants came and handed me the phone. When I got the news, tears rushed to my eyes, and when I turned around to catch my breath, my friend was standing there to hold me. In one moment, David caught me when I was falling and gave me the strength to finish taping.

Another time I really needed my friend was when my mother's Alzheimer's got worse. We had just finished our first recording with Kirk Franklin and the Family, and at this point we were starting to make a little noise in the industry. But my mother never understood what was going on. We would come home and say, "Hey, Momma, we are going to be on TV!" She would look at us as if she didn't even know what a television was. It was a painful moment to see the woman who had prayed for you to succeed now unable to witness your success.

It was my mother who told me, "Always love the Lord with all of your heart and the Lord will take you far." But when the time came for her words to come true, she was too far away in her mind to comprehend what was happening. In times like these I needed more than a husband. I needed my friend. David's constant support through my mother's sickness was the stabilizer I needed just to get up the next day and keep on going. He was strength to my weakness, and he always offered me a better way of seeing things.

The busier we became, the more accommodations David made for me to be with my mother as often as possible. David moved my mother in with us, and we took care of her the best we knew how until she moved in with my sister. I watched my vibrant mother shift from being the most encouraging, loving, and kind woman I knew to not remembering how to feed herself or go to the restroom on her own. All of her dreams were coming to pass. When I sang at Carnegie Hall, I thought of my mother. But she couldn't come to be a part of it. And worst of all, I couldn't tell her. Some nights I would sit beside her bed and just talk to her, hoping that she would talk back to me. But she didn't say a word. It was so painful, but my friend was right by my side. I would cry onstage and weep at the mere thought of my mother, Mary. No one else but David knew how to translate my tears and encourage me through the pain. He is the wind beneath my wings. He always knew what to say to make me smile. When I felt my heart leap out of my chest, he would say something funny and make me laugh while I was crying. That's what friends are for.

If you ask me what my one word of advice would be for couples who are thinking about getting married, I would echo the words of my husband—focus on building a friendship. As Christians, David and I built our marriage on our faith—our Lord and Savior—first and foremost. But directly after that, it's all about our friendship. Everything else falls in place under that. David has proven to me every day, over and over again, that there is, indeed, a friend that sticks closer than a brother. He's seen me overwhelmed and afraid, and he still loves me.

She's stood in my corner on my worst days, and she still loves me.

If we are eating a meal from the dollar menu of a fast-food restaurant or in the banquet hall of the White House, my friend is there with me.

If we are walking the streets of a new country or feeding the poor, my friend is there with me.

When I buried my mom and sang at my loved ones' funerals, my friend was there with me.

When shows were canceled, and people who promised to be there walked away and never called back, my friend was there with me.

Whenever it got tough in my marriage, I would always draw from my friendship account with Tam. Our friendship developed into genuine love for one another; a love that doesn't want to live without her; a love that doesn't want a good thing to happen unless she knows; a love that is loyal, meaningful, true, and real. It's that love that I drew from when the going got tough. And trust me, times did get tough. There were days when Tam pushed my patience to the limit, and I'm sure there were days when I did the same. But the foundation of our marriage as friends helped us to love the unlikeable parts of each other. I love the whole person that I see when I see Tamela Mann. And she loves the whole person that she sees when she sees me. If she hurts my feelings or if I disappoint her, we have learned how to get through it together because a friend who loves is a friend who forgives.

A FRIEND LOVES AND A FRIEND FORGIVES

It's easy for me to forgive Tam when I remind myself that my spouse is on the same team as me. We collaborate. We cooperate. And we trust each other no matter what. I know that Tam would never do anything to hurt me intentionally, so if I am hurting because of her, I have learned to ask myself a new question: Where is she hurting because of me?

The same questions can be explored in your marriage. Maybe you have nothing to do with their pain. Maybe something outside of your marriage has been causing them pain for a long time. Maybe they are hostile because they've had to manage life on their own for so long. Maybe they did not receive the fundamental things that every child needs: attention, affection, affirmation, acceptance, and encouragement. If they did not receive those things, maybe they don't know how to give them.

I can tell you from experience: It's hard to give what you've never had. It's hard to learn a lesson you've never been taught. I didn't have a father to show me how to be a man. I had a lot of brothers, but a lot of times we had to figure it out. My father didn't show me how to say "I'm sorry" before he passed away. I never heard those words from him. As a result, I was hurt, and I didn't know I was hurt. In the same way, your spouse may be hurting in a way that they don't know is affecting your marriage. And if hurt people hurt people, then broken people break people.

Tam and I now forgive each other more easily because we've learned to look for each other's broken places. I try to listen for the places in her heart where the bleeding stopped but the pain continued. I know it had to hurt Tam to be picked on as a child. I know a lot of people made fun of her and ridiculed her for several reasons. Her family didn't graduate from school. She didn't have a skinny model-like shape. And just growing up where we grew up lended itself to a lot of unnecessary criticism. Understanding that part of Tam's history changed my sensitivity when speaking to her. I learned to lighten up on certain topics so as not to push buttons that would ultimately cause Tam to become offended. It also helped to apologize quicker because I learned that, unbeknownst to me, my words were triggering memories from a pain that I didn't cause.

> **I try to listen for the places in her heart where the bleeding stopped but the pain continued.**

Every husband needs to be willing to fix a pain they did not inflict. Many couples take their pain out on the person who loves them because they can't take it out on the person who hurt them. Sometimes it's not your fault, and other times it is. That's the truth.

But most often, we are sent to our wives to heal a pain we did not cause. Our sensitivity to their pain and our willingness to apologize makes healing a reality in our marriages.

PLAN FOR THE PAIN

I have a medicine cabinet in our home. Inside that cabinet is a first-aid kit, a few Band-Aids, some aspirin (for if we get a headache), and some cough medicine (for if we get sick). Even if we aren't sick at the moment, many of us buy medicine while we are feeling well just in case sickness happens. Why? Because no matter how healthy you may be today, no one is exempt from catching a cold tomorrow. I've learned it's wise to plan for the pains that come up in marriage too.

Most of us have a plan for our passion. We even have a plan for our pleasure. But we don't have a plan for our pain. Every marriage will have all three. Every marriage will experience sunshine, rainbows, full moons, and beautiful sunrises. There will be times when you look at your man and say, "Mmm, you look so good!" There will be times when he will look at you and think, *What did I do to deserve such a wonderful woman?* Then there are times when you will look at him and think, *What was I thinking when I said, "I do"?* This is life. Every marriage will experience high mountains and low valleys. Every marriage will experience volcanic eruptions, a hurricane here or there, an unexpected earthquake, and thunderstorms when you least expect them. But your job is to figure out what you will do when the weather changes.

Think back on the last time the weather changed in your marriage. What happened that caused the love to shift? What happened that caused the earth to shake? How long did the honeymoon phase last, and when did it change? When did you realize that your marriage went from bright and sunny to cloudy with a chance of rain? When you figure out what caused the weather to change, then you can prepare yourself to put on the right clothes, depending on the season your marriage is in.

MANAGING YOUR BAGGAGE

Often we model in our marriage what we experienced as children growing up. If your dad was an avoider, then you will probably do the same. If your mother was a yeller, then you will probably do the same. If your parents never yelled, then yelling might indicate a larger issue than truly exists.

Tam and I had a huge blowup about our dog. The dog had bitten someone and was causing problems in the neighborhood. Our neighbors called the pound, and when the dogcatcher showed up, Tam told them they could take him. Naturally, I got upset about it. We ended up having a huge argument over the situation.

David went back and forth through the house, carrying on about how upset he was about this dog. It wasn't that serious to me, but I didn't like the way he was dragging the point out, so I got louder as he got louder. By the end of the night we had forgiven each other, apologized, and made up. But unbeknownst to us, Tia heard us yelling at each other, so she ran into her other siblings' room, upset. By the time she opened her mouth, she was hysterical. She said, "What we gonna do?"

They said, "Tia, what are you talking about?"

She said, "Mom and Dad are getting a divorce!"

The kids had no clue what made her say that, so they all started panicking. Tia wanted to know where the kids were going to live, who was going to move in with Momma and who was going to stay with me. She wanted to know if we had to move out of our home and go to different schools. She had so many questions and so few answers. Tia wasn't used to hearing us argue, so it caused her to think something was terribly wrong. Often kids become desensitized when they hear arguments constantly. But her mind was made up: we were getting a divorce because she saw an argument and never heard the apology.

When we realized what was going on, we explained that we had just had a disagreement, and we weren't going to get a divorce. We apologized to her and we apologized to the rest of the family. So in addition to us saying "I'm sorry" to each other, we learned the importance of resolving our conflict in front of our families as well. If your children see you upset at one another, then they also need to see you forgive one another. If not, they will carry the guilt or blame or pain of an argument already resolved, and that has the potential to ruin their perception of a healthy marriage. I said all of that to say, it really does matter what you model in your home. It matters what rules you put in place because what you do and what you don't do will have an effect on your children.

Tam and I thought we were doing a good job of hiding our disagreements from our children, but if we didn't learn how to forgive in their presence, they would form an idea about relationships that wasn't true. We wanted them to know that conflicts arise. We wanted them to know that sometimes Mommy and Daddy disagree. But we also wanted them to see that forgiveness is possible and every disagreement doesn't have to end in divorce.

I agree with David 100 percent. How you resolve conflict in the household is so important. What is also important with regard to forgiveness is ridding yourself of pride in order to learn how to say "I'm sorry" without your spouse telling you, "This or that hurt me."

This was a lesson that took me a long time to figure out! In the beginning of our relationship, it was difficult for me to say, "I was wrong." I felt degraded when I said it. It made me feel like I was wrong about everything, all the time. But the truth is, I was afraid to be vulnerable. I liked feeling as if I had it all together. When I admitted my failures, it made me feel weak. It made me feel less than.

But now David says "I'm sorry" quicker than he makes a mistake. He apologizes for things he didn't do to make sure he's not justifying himself for things he did do. That, to me, shows the level of growth he has achieved on his own.

I can only attribute that growth to my willingness to walk away from the stereotypes about manhood that I grew up buying into. Sometimes the world will make you feel like you have to be perfect, strong, and effortless all the time, but that's not true. If you look at commercials on television, you see strong men and athletic men. Men are supposed to have it together. Men are supposed to know what to do. Men are never supposed to lose control. We are problem solvers; and most times that is true. But we don't know how to do everything. We can't fix every situation. Often we need to give ourselves permission to fail. Our wives are sent to fix things we can't fix, to help in ways that we can't. When I fail to see my flaws, pride gets in the way. I walk around as if everything hinges on my abilities, and that's not true.

If you don't fix pride now, pride will have you in pain and unable to move forward! Ask me how I know. One time I got upset with Tam about something, and I decided not to talk to her for the rest of the day. We got in the car. I didn't say a word. We got to the grocery store. I didn't say a word. I made sure to create enough distance between me and her in the supermarket so that people knew I wasn't talking to her, and she didn't have to talk to me. I was mad! I wanted her to feel it so she could get the point. So I shut down.

What I didn't expect was for my hips to shut down too. I was walking down aisle 2 next to the milk section, and my hip joints locked up like the Tin Man from *The Wizard of Oz*. I remember waking up that morning with a little pain in my hips, and all day they had been bothering me a little bit. But when I got to the store, my hips just locked up. I was in so much pain, and all I could do was stand there like a statue. I literally could not move a bone in my body until the pain passed. Tamela was right there, feet away from me, but I would not utter a mumbling word. I told myself, *If I die, let me die*, but I wasn't gonna say one word to her!

And I didn't.

And she kept shopping.

And I was in pain to the point of tears, and she didn't know.

HIDDEN PAIN

When I told Tam later that day about my hips locking up, we laughed for days. We laughed because I was one conversation away from getting the help I needed, but pride wouldn't let me ask for help.

I wonder how many wives are oblivious to a pain they don't know about because of their husband's pride. Keeping silent about our pain, we rob them of a chance to give us a helping hand.

This is the lesson I learned: never let pride prevent you from loving each other and apologizing to one another. Even if you've spoken about the same situation in the past, don't allow past reactions to get in the way of your present feelings. If you go to the doctor and don't tell him what's wrong, the doctor will almost always misdiagnose your problem. If you expect your spouse to just figure it out, you are setting them up to fail.

When pride rules a relationship, silence is the consequence.

When pride rules a relationship, silence is the consequence. Nobody talks. Nobody wants to fix anything. You walk around the house upset at each other, and you know she's upset because she yells "I'm fine!" at the top of her lungs. She also drags her feet to let you know she's not fine.

Your husband, on the other hand, is definitely not okay because he buries himself in work and disappears to his man cave without saying a word.

She occupies her time with the kids, and when you get in the bed together, you move all the way to the edge of the bed so you don't have to touch each other. After a while you decide to sleep on the couch. Then you decide to stay at a friend's house. Next thing you know, you're talking about divorce because pride came in to tear apart your marriage. Pride wants to keep you from telling each other the truth. But it doesn't have to be that way. Decide to be the bigger person. Have the hard conversation. Think about the end result, and if the topic is too hard to address one-on-one, talk to someone who can help you to identify the root behind the offense.

PRIDE GOES BOTH WAYS

Men aren't the only people who battle with pride, ladies. Sometimes we can walk around thinking we are flawless, and we live as if nobody can tell us we are wrong. This is not the way to conduct a healthy marriage. Living like that creates a hostile love environment. Either people are afraid to tell you the truth or they tell the truth but say it to everyone else but you.

Have you ever had food stuck in your teeth, and everyone laughed about it but nobody told you it was there? Love tells you the truth. Love tells you when your attitude is out of alignment. David knows me. He knows I don't want him to go out in the world thinking everything is okay when it's not. I'd rather tell him the truth in private than for him to be humiliated in public.

Unlike David, I didn't have a problem saying I'm wrong because I grew up thinking I was wrong about everything. But when David came along, he taught me balance. He taught me how to speak up for myself and how to express my real feelings. I didn't know how to express myself at first. All I knew was that I hated tension in our home. I wanted to say what we needed to say right away and move on! Sometimes I would raise my voice when I felt like David wasn't hearing me, but now I have figured out what his triggers are. I know how to approach him when he's wrong, and I know how to admit when I'm wrong. Most of all, I know how to say, "Honey, please forgive me."

"THEY KNOW NOT WHAT THEY DO"

There will be times when you won't want to ask for forgiveness because you honestly don't feel like you've done anything wrong. But forgiveness is not about being right; it's about giving up your right to be right. Forgiveness is about letting go of the small stuff and putting everything in its proper perspective.

When the doctors told David I needed major surgery, we suddenly realized that some things weren't that serious. We forgot about the small stuff and started focusing on what really mattered. Some things that I used to hold grudges about I let go of. Some things that I used to think were major were actually really minor. At the end of the day, your marriage is about persevering through the difficult days.

When your spouse is in a hospital bed, or when the doctor gives you a startling diagnosis, you'll quickly see what matters in your relationship. I'm not saying you don't have a right to feel how you feel, but always ask yourself, "Is what I'm upset about really that serious in the end?" Is the thing you are carrying worth carrying? Is this something you can get through together?

David and I are both living witnesses of the forgiving power of Jesus. David has hurt me, and I have hurt him. But through prayer and consistent time with the Lord, we were able to survive the worst of storms. Remember that when you say, "I do," you give up the ability to live as an independent contractor. You are one with your spouse. You will make decisions together, make memories together, raise children together, work hard together, and forgive one another together.

Whenever I struggle with forgiveness, I remember the words of Jesus: "Father, forgive them, for they know not what they do" (Luke 23:34). I understand those words better now that I have children. No question about it, I love all of my children with all of my heart. And I know my children love me with all of their hearts. But when they were toddlers, I couldn't give them everything I wanted to give them, even if I was giving it out of love.

Imagine if I gave one of my children a check written out for a large amount of money. At two or three years old, children don't really know what to do with a check, so they would probably rip it up or turn it into a ball to play with. Even if I gave them the check to express my love, they wouldn't know how to value my gift because they are not mature enough to appreciate it. If they rip it up, I can only laugh. Why? Because they don't know what they are doing. They don't understand the value of the thing that is in their hand.

In the same way, sometimes I've learned to extend grace to David during moments when he just doesn't understand the big picture of what he is doing. Sometimes we write metaphorical checks to our spouse to express our love when they haven't grown in a certain area to understand it or appreciate it. Sometimes they do understand what they are doing and they do intend to hurt you. If that is the case, then only Jesus (and counseling) can change them. But if your spouse did not mean to hurt you, then it's much easier to forgive them.

Today I hope that you will ask the Lord for a new perspective. Maybe, just maybe, they didn't know what they were doing. Maybe, just maybe, God is going to give you new grace and new mercy to see each other differently. Life is too short to major on the minor stuff. Forgive today. Forgive forever.

WILL YOU PRAY WITH US?

*Father, help us to see each other the way you see us. You for-
gave us while we were at our worst. Give us the grace to forgive
each other until we reach our best. We can't do this without you.
We love you and we love each other. Show us the big picture.
Reveal the root to every issue. Thank you for our friendship.
Thank you for my spouse, who reminds me that there is a friend
that sticks closer than a brother. When we feel overwhelmed,
remind us of our never-ending bond and love for each other.
Help us to remember the memories that brought us together
and not the mistakes that tore us apart. In Jesus' name, amen.*

DISCUSSION QUESTIONS

1. What do you love the most about your friend (spouse)?
   What do you admire the most about your friend?
2. Recall a memory that constantly reminds you of the
   beauty of your friendship with your spouse.
3. Share a time when your spouse offered support to you in
   a special way. (Perhaps they don't know how important
   their presence was to you during that time.)
4. What can you do to revive the friendship in your
   marriage? Develop a plan and work on it together.
5. When is the last time you forgave your spouse?
6. When is the last time you've said, "I was wrong"?
7. When you forgive, do you forgive and let it go, or do you
   forgive and rehearse?

8. As a child, how did you see forgiveness modeled in your home?

9. As a child, what needs (affection, attention, affirmation, encouragement) were neglected that you may be searching to fill in your marriage?

BONUS ACTIVITY: WORKING ON FORGIVENESS TOGETHER

Ever heard of a vision board? We want to challenge you to create a *forgiveness* board. You can start it below and finish it in a journal or on your computer. Here's the question: What has pride or shame kept you from saying or admitting to yourself that you need to say? What haven't you forgiven God about? What haven't you forgiven yourself about? In what area do you need to forgive your spouse? Use this board to reflect on the pain you may have experienced and to release yourself from unforgiveness.

FORGIVENESS BOARD

God	
Myself	
My Spouse	

After you have written your words on the forgiveness board, choose one of those areas and write a letter to free yourself from the grip of unforgiveness. If you're upset with God, write a letter to God. If you haven't released yourself from a mistake you made in the past, write a letter discussing the struggle you are facing and why. Finally, if you are struggling to forgive your spouse, write a letter to them and free them from the pain they've caused you. You do not have to share this letter. You may want to share it with your spouse after you have processed how you feel. But take your time and write it so you can begin to heal.

_____

_____

_____

_____

_____

_____

_____

_____

CHAPTER 17

LOL TOGETHER

Laughing and Loving Out Loud

Couples who laugh together last together.
—DR. JOHN GOTTMANN

I f I had to sum up life with David, I'd say it's all about LOL. We laugh out loud, and we love out loud. Truly, we have so much fun as a married couple! First of all, he is hilarious, and second of all, David is fresh! Either he's trying to make me laugh or he's trying to have sex.

KEEPING IT FRESH

Nothing wrong with that, right, Tam? We keep it fresh and fun.

Marriage should always be filled with joy and passion. I'm always surprised when married couples don't laugh out loud together. In fact, in my experience, a lot of folks laugh with their friends, but not with their spouse. I'm not sure why this is, but if I had to guess, I think a lot of people take life too seriously. When the bills come and the children come, and the responsibilities grow, we stop laughing. We stop enjoying one another. But I believe it is possible to change the climate of your household with one minor adjustment—your decision to LOL often.

THE POWER OF LAUGHTER

Absolutely! One of the greatest joys of my life is watching David on tour. There will be thousands of people in the audience cracking up, and they just don't want David to leave the stage during his comedy set. Somehow he's found a way to tap in to the joy their lives have stolen. He's found a way to minister to everyone's broken places. The beauty of David's mind is that he knows the right things to say to reassure people who have lost their hope.

Every time I watch him onstage, I walk away knowing everything is going to be all right. In our marriage we have discovered that sometimes the best counseling session for us is a big dose of laughter. Sometimes David and I don't need to talk, we just need to laugh. Laughter is medicine to our souls. Laughter helps to break up the tough stuff. Laughter is one way to break the ice when things are feeling cold in the home.

Sex is another way.

I know, David. We'll get to that in a minute. As I was saying, laughter reminds couples to be playful and fun-loving. Life is too short.

Tam, you are so right. Who wants to look at the Grinch all the time? Have you ever met someone who was so mean, they didn't even like spending time with themselves? Many marriages suffer because we haven't yet understood the importance of balancing the serious things in life with joy. Tam and I love the Lord. But we also know how to have fun. We know how to spend time with family, dance together, and share together, and then go and worship when it's time to worship. To everything there is a season.

What I love about Tam is that she's still that person I run to and tell good news to. Do you still have that friend to whom you send funny clips from social media? Can you laugh out loud with your spouse and

It's never too late to revive the laughter. The joy is worth it!

enjoy each other without any extra fanfare? It's never too late to revive the laughter. The joy is worth it! I'm telling you—most of the things Tam and I argue about, we end up laughing over.

The stories are endless when I think about how true that statement is! David, do you remember when you were getting to know my likes and dislikes?

I do. I think one of the most memorable stories is the Big Gulp!

Early on in our marriage, we were still getting to know things about each other. David knew I drank Dr. Pepper every once in a while, and he knew I liked different flavors of juice, but he didn't know my usual drink. So one hot day in Texas, we were driving on an empty highway. I was pregnant at the time. David stopped at a 7-Eleven, and I asked for something refreshing to drink.

I hollered back, "Refreshing drink, coming right up!" It was so hot, I couldn't wait to get inside the air-conditioned store. But when I got inside, I realized I didn't know what to get her. I figured I would get her a Big Gulp. The Big Gulp was a thirty-two-ounce humongous drink. They had several different flavors from which to choose—cherry, strawberry, Coke, etc.—and I didn't want to walk outside to ask her which flavor she wanted. So I got all of the flavors in one drink. We call that a "suicide" in Texas. I knew she would love it. I put each flavor in the drink in equal proportions. Then I fixed myself a drink, paid for them, and walked back to the car.

When I got in the car, poor Tam was sweating bullets. The temperature must've gone up by ten degrees, and she may have been a bit hormonal. I handed my sweetheart the drink that I had worked so hard to make for her. She tasted it one time and looked at me with the ugly church face.

"What kind of drink is this?"

I said, "It's a suicide. I got you a little bit of everything because I didn't know what you wanted."

Tam looked at me with the look of pure death and said to me, *"I don't want no suicide!"*

How ungrateful, I thought. I looked at her and then I decided to do something that she didn't see coming. I took her drink and threw it straight out of the window! Before she knew it, the Big Gulp was out on the highway.

I was shocked. How in the world did David think it was okay to throw my drink out the window? I thought about how I should react. Of course I could've reacted lovingly and calmly, but I was pregnant, and I was thirsty, and now I was hot with David! So I decided to one-up him.

She took my drink and proceeded to throw it out of the window on her side of the car. In a flash she threw the drink, and she just knew she had paid me back for what I did. The problem is, Tam's window was still rolled up. The drink bounced off the glass and bounced back onto her face! Everything was wet. Her hair, her face, her clothes. Everything!

Talk about LOL! We rode all the way down the road laughing at how much a fool we had made of ourselves. Clearly we weren't really upset with each other. We were just reacting emotionally when we should have just paused, admitted our feelings, and handled the problem like adults. Instead we just made a mess and then laughed. That laughter was worth it!

I agree, Tam. And what I love about our marriage is we will do anything to make each other laugh! Do you remember when I tricked you with the apple pie?

Oh yeah. How can I forget?! The apple pie!

Get this. One night after church Tam and I both had a taste for apple pie, so we drove to McDonald's, got a few burgers, and then ordered two apple pies. They were closing when we pulled up, and they only had one apple pie left. They gave us a cherry pie free of charge to make up for the inconvenience. Now, personally, I hate cherry pie, and I didn't want to share my apple pie, so I ate the apple pie, then I switched the boxes so that the cherry pie was waiting for Tam to eat it from the apple pie box. I wanted to see how Tam would react, thinking it was apple pie only to realize it was cherry. She almost caught on 'cause I kept rushing her to finish her burger so I could see her reaction. She was taking all day!

When she finally finished eating her burger, I watched her open the box with joy and excitement. I saw her close her eyes to get ready for this apple pie delight. I saw her chomp down on that pie until cherry juice sat right on the side of her lip. In those two seconds between her biting into the pie, tasting it, and then seeing red on her lips, her face went through nineteen different emotions. She was surprised, shocked, confused, mad . . . I was on the floor rolling! Tam was about to spit the pie out but she couldn't. When she finally finished the first bite, she looked at me and said, "You play too much! Seriously, David, somebody is going to hurt you."

I still think this is my all-time greatest practical joke ever. Tam didn't think it was funny at first, but then we laughed and laughed and laughed. But all of this was fun and games.

We have had so many opportunities to smile and laugh together over the years that it's become a habit. I know every marriage works differently, but I promised Tam, a long time ago, that I would keep her smiling to keep her from crying. I never wanted us to get so serious about life that we forgot to laugh. I never wanted to turn our marriage into the courtroom. Sure, every husband wants to be respected and every wife wants the same, but no one should be so intimidating that their presence makes others nervous around them. I don't want my wife trembling or shrinking whenever I walk in the room. Listen, I am a clown all by myself. I am not ashamed to laugh at myself or make a fool of myself. Part of keeping our marriage fresh means being willing to do silly things, take funny pictures, laugh until we cry, and enjoy each other's company through every situation and in every circumstance.

LOVE OUT LOUD

Let's switch gears from laughing to grinning. It's time to talk about ways to keep the fire burning in your marriage. When it comes to sex, I have learned a lot about what Tam needs as a woman. My wife needs to be touched. She doesn't just want to rush to sex. She wants foreplay. She wants attention. She wants me to whisper sweet nothings in her ear and say things to her to get her in the mood. For me, I'm different. Some days, there's a blaring alarm inside of me screaming, "Sex! Sex! Sex!" I don't need to be warmed up. I don't need to be talked into it. I don't need you to do anything but grant me access, my beautiful queen.

David!

What, Momma? I'm telling the truth. But Tam is a little different. Intimacy with Tam is about the journey. So, along the way, Tam wants to sight-see and stop multiple times in order to explore the trees and lakes we are passing by. I, on the other hand, don't mind skipping past the rest stops and getting to our final destination as soon as possible.

See, Tam taught me the difference between intimacy and intercourse. My idea of intimacy was to smack Tam on the behind and hope she would like it. Then I would give her my smoothest line so she knew I was coming on to her. But the flirtatious gesture would fall flat on the floor. She didn't respond the way I wanted her to. Later, when I started to pay attention, I noticed that when I touched Tam with no hidden agenda, that was when she would get the most turned on. If I simply held her hand in the car, or if I brushed the side of her back while passing by her in the house, Tam would be stimulated in ways I didn't realize. A few hours later she would respond in a way that showed me: I was meeting her needs as well.

Now I make it a habit to touch her in a way that gets her attention, even if it doesn't necessarily meet my immediate need. The goal in sex is to please her. If I do that well, then she will please me well. Whenever I am close to her, I make it a point to touch her in the way she enjoys, and MANN . . . am I rewarded! It has become such a habit that sometimes I forget I'm not supposed to touch her in the middle of church! I know it's not a good place to cop a feel, and I know it's inappropriate on many levels, but sometimes, when I think on all the Lord has blessed me with, I just can't help myself.

Lord, help my husband. Sisters, let me be honest with you. When David and I were just learning each other sexually, I didn't always know how to communicate my sexual needs to him. Like David said, I wanted to be caressed. I wanted a hug after work. I felt like David was ignoring me, and I wanted him to see me. Now that I have matured and now that David and I have learned to talk about everything, including sex, I tell him the truth no matter what. David knows me and I know him. I know his sexual appetite. And because he is my husband, I enjoy fulfilling his needs. I enjoy figuring out ways to keep the intimacy fresh in our marriage.

Many times, David and I have told the kids we were going to the store, and on the way back, we got a room at the cheapest motel you could imagine and enjoyed one another without interruption. The fire must stay in our marriage, so we've learned to improvise when things become dull. Sometimes I've found that just going into another room, or changing it up a little bit in the bedroom so he doesn't know what I'm going to do, will enhance our sex life.

I want to be David's wife, his girlfriend on the side, and everything in between. Many Christians don't like to talk about this in church, but I believe that neglect is one of the primary reasons infidelity happens. When a person feels neglected, they are vulnerable to distraction. When a husband or wife feels neglected, they become vulnerable to temptation. My mother used to say,

"Tamela, be aware of the tricks of the Enemy. Don't be ignorant to Satan's devices. He wants to destroy your marriage, and he won't stop until you are unhappy and unsatisfied." Thank you, Momma. She always kept it real. That's why I loved her!

And in the sex area, keeping it real has become a big issue because no matter how spiritual you are, church attendance can't fix a bedroom problem. Shouting can't fix a bedroom problem. Reading more Scripture can't fix a bedroom problem. In order to restore the flame of love and intimacy in your marriage, you may need to go to counseling. You may be feeling like he doesn't communicate with you, and he may be feeling like you communicate too much. You may feel nervous and uncertain about what to do and how to do it. There are a million things that couples feel when it comes to sex, and I don't have the answers for everything, but one thing I do know is this: issues aren't fixed by being silent about them. In order for anything to change, both parties should be willing to have the hard conversation.

> I want to be David's wife, his girlfriend on the side, and everything in between.

Different people need different forms of touch. Some people like to hold hands with their spouse. Some are a lot more private with their affection. Some love getting their backs rubbed while sitting at the movies or playing footsie at the table. Others are uncomfortable with public displays of affection. No matter the preference, Tam has taught me that we all have different needs based on who we are. As her husband, I have made it my full-time job to pay attention to her nonverbal desires as well as her verbal requests so that ultimately she is satisfied emotionally, physically, and any other way that I can please her.

WHERE HAS ALL THE KISSING GONE?

Go back to the very beginning of your relationship. Remember what things were like back then? Touch is no different. Think about what forms of touch connected you two in the first place. When you were first dating, there were ways your spouse touched you that built intimacy and formed a bond. You didn't just go from saying hi and shaking hands to jumping in the bed one day. No, there were some kinds of touch that you two did over time that opened those doors that built that connection. Remember those touches that brought you together and eventually ended up in a sexual relationship. The brushing of hands that led to hand-holding and hugging, and then kissing, and more. It was a process. Touching increased and got more intense over time, and that was part of the way that you two got comfortable enough with each other to move to more intimate acts. Well, guess what? These are still an essential part of marriage, no matter how long you two have been together. These are still the steps that lead to sexual intimacy, but some people forget that. After a while, for instance, many married couples experience a decrease in kissing just for the sake of kissing. Eventually in some marriages, kissing is only present during lovemaking, which in my opinion is so backward because kissing is one of those small physical tokens that make a world of difference during sexual intimacy.

You'd be surprised how many couples couldn't keep their hands off each other before marriage, but barely touch each other now that they are married. This is a trick of the Enemy to keep intimacy far away from your covenant. The Enemy knows that intimacy can break down walls. Connection with your spouse can improve communication. Making love to your spouse allows you to connect with them in a way that you can't connect with anyone else.

If you have lost a desire to be with your spouse and you need some help, seek it. Talk to your pastor or counselor about it, and communicate together. If there has been unfaithfulness in your marriage and that has interrupted the intimacy, seek counsel together. These are not easy issues to get through, but they are not impossible issues to get through. With God all things are possible. If your spouse does not know how to satisfy you in the bedroom, the best way to fix it is to face it. Silence doesn't fix the problem; most times it exacerbates it. Talk up. Speak up. And, most importantly, have a lot of fun and keep the fire burning.

WILL YOU PRAY WITH US?

God of compassion, God of love, you ordained intimacy to bring us closer together. You ordained physical connection to keep us attracted to one another. Help us to grow in our connection. You also created love, joy, and laughter to remind us not to take life too seriously. Laughter is medicine for the soul, and we pray that you will help us to nurture a loving, peaceful marriage that brings joy in our home. Help us to be honest about our needs, and give us eyes only for each other. In Jesus' name, amen.

DISCUSSION QUESTIONS

1. How important is fun in your marriage on a scale from 1 to 10 (10 being extremely important)?

2. When is the last time you and your spouse laughed together until you cried?

3. On a stressful day, what is your ideal way to unplug? What gives you personal joy?

4. How often do you pull away from the work and the responsibilities to just have a good time?

5. What is the primary thing hindering you from having a fun, joy-filled marriage? What can you do to enhance the joy in your marriage?

6. How often do you kiss each other? Are you satisfied with the frequency of that affection?

7. What can you do to improve the intimacy in your relationship? Answer the question first, and then ask your spouse what you can do to enhance the intimacy?

8. What do each of you believe about sex and intimacy in your relationship? How do you understand the intersection between sex and faith?

9. How can you include your spouse in helping you to unplug?

10. Challenge: Kiss every day in a different way! Challenge yourselves to spend seven days loving on your spouse (physically) the way they desire to be loved.

BONUS ACTIVITY: JOY BAROMETER

Think about things in your marriage that give you joy. Think about the fun times and reflect on the different memories that have kept the fun fresh in your marriage. Fill in the following chart:

HUSBAND	WIFE
My happiest moment with you was when we	My happiest moment with you was when we
My funniest memory of you when we started dating was	My funniest memory of you when we started dating was
My face lights up when you	My face lights up when you
My favorite picture of you is (find the picture and show your spouse)	My favorite picture of you is (find the picture and show your spouse)

The craziest thing we ever did as a couple was	The craziest thing we ever did as a couple was
The funniest movie I've ever seen is (watch it this week with your spouse)	The funniest movie I've ever seen is (watch it this week with your spouse)

CHAPTER 18

FAITH

It Begins and Ends with Jesus

> *It is my conviction that marriage is such a good
> idea, only God could have thought of it.*
>
> —MYLES MUNROE

When people ask us how Tam and I have made it to where we are today, there is really only one answer: *Jesus*. Because of our faith in Jesus, we have seen miracles in our marriage. Because of our faith in him, we have been able to encourage one another through anything.

David is absolutely right. Jesus is the center of it all for us. The music, the stage, the awards, the ratings, the ups, the downs—all of it has been wonderful, but the truth is, none of it would've mattered—or even have been possible—without God. No amount of success or fame matters unless it glorifies God. David and I have tried to teach our children this since they were born, and we try our best to be examples of God's love in the world. What we have is not because of us. Our journey is all because of Jesus. Without him we are nothing. Because of him, we can do anything.

WHEN ALL ELSE FAILS: JESUS

I'll never forget what happened when our youngest child, Tia, turned two years old. She was sick, and at first we thought she had a common cold. Despite our efforts she was not getting any better. Then her illness got worse, so we thought it was the flu. Her condition grew worse and worse, so we took her to the hospital. By that point we were scared. She was crying with no tears, and she wasn't urinating. Doctors evaluated her and said she had an infection and was severely dehydrated. Without immediate intervention she would die. These are words no mother or father should ever have to hear.

David had to hold baby Tia while they put an IV needle into her small body. Negative thoughts began to plague me. I thought, *Babies die from illnesses like this.* But the peace of God entered into the room. David looked and me and said, "We've got to trust God." He was right! The situation was out of our control, but God was in control. While Tia was in that hospital room, I prayed like never before. I believe God heard our prayers and healed our daughter. Prayer still works! God is faithful.

I can't speak to everybody else's experience, but that incident is just one of many—prayer has been essential in our marriage. I can't stress enough how important prayer is to the health of anyone's marriage. Prayer is the key to living a peaceful life with God. Prayer is the root of our communication with God. It is the way we connect to heaven. And when life seems impossible, the confidence David and I have is in this one undeniable truth: God hears us. God hears our cry, and God hears our needs. He has never stopped listening to us. Knowing that has helped me to get through the rough days when I just wanted to let it all go.

God hears our cry, and God hears our needs. He has never stopped listening to us.

And to those reading, let me encourage you. I know it gets hard sometimes, but God provides. He will never leave you nor forsake you. When you feel overwhelmed, go to God. God knows what you really need. He made your husband. He knows his flaws. He made you. He knows your flaws. Even if you don't know what to do, God will guide you and direct you so that you can help each other and not hurt each other.

THE BEST MARRIAGES BEGIN AT THE FEET OF JESUS

It all begins with the King. Tam and I have no doubt that Jesus is the reason we are still in love today. And I believe if you are reading this book and you do not have a relationship with Christ, the best decision you could make is to turn to Jesus. Your marriage can be good if you don't pray, but it can be great when you do pray. Your marriage can be good if you don't know the Lord, but it can be great when you do know the Lord. A threefold cord is not easily broken. When God is in the middle of your marriage, and when you both are committed to developing a relationship with Christ, the two of you can survive any storm. You can overcome any obstacle.

Honestly, I don't know where I would be if I didn't have a wife who prayed for me. I don't know who I would be if I didn't have a relationship with God. One of my new favorite songs to hear Tam sing is a song called "The Potter." The message of the song is simple: God is the Potter. We are the clay, so, as the clay, we just need to learn to let him have his way. We need to let him have his way in our marriage. We need to let him have his way in our home. Sure, it may hurt for a moment, but when God works on you, you will never be the same.

LET GOD LEAD

A lifestyle of prayer is not easy. It is far from easy, but I will tell you, it is better to let God lead than to live without him. God is not a man that he should lie. He may test your faith and test your marriage, but he will always produce a treasure from the trial. And if you think it's hard without children, just wait until babies start coming! As our children grew up, we had to learn to trust God on a whole new level.

I mean, let's face it, all of us worry from time to time. But prayer turns worry into worship. Prayer turns sorrow into joy. Prayer allows you to pour your heart out to God, and as you do that, he strengthens you in the middle of your weakest day. I'm telling you what I know! As a parent, it was difficult to see my children make decisions that seemed to be in the opposite direction of God's plan, but I had to take my hands off it. I had to trust God through it all. Surely, if you let God lead your life, he will cover those you love.

I've seen God move time and time again. And my family isn't perfect, but we are learning to let God drive the car, steer the ship, and lead the family. No matter where you are in your journey, learn to trust in Jesus. Learn to trust in God. If you do, he will help you to get through it all. "Be strong and courageous. Do not be afraid or terrified because of them, for the LORD your God goes with you; he will never leave you nor forsake you" (Deuteronomy 31:6 NIV).

GOD WILL HELP YOU THROUGH IT

No matter what you're going through, God will help you through it. Your story may not be our story. Your situation may be totally different from ours. Every marriage has its ups and downs. Every marriage will encounter a surprise at the door that you both did not expect. But the Lord will be the bridge over your troubled waters. The Lord will help you when you have no one else to call on. Never forget that. God is with you in your marriage. God is for you. God will never leave you nor forsake you. God wants you to win through this. Even if it gets hard, know this: you are not by yourself. Sometimes you will get upset with him. Sometimes he will get upset with you. But God is with you both. He is there to help you, strengthen you, encourage you, and give you the strength to do better tomorrow.

> **Feelings will change. Beauty will change. Money will change. Excitement will disappear. But Jesus will keep you even when you want to walk away.**

Feelings will change. Beauty will change. Money will change. Excitement will disappear. But Jesus will keep you even when you want to walk away. Jesus will help you even when times get rough. The greater your relationship with Christ, the more strength your marriage will have. Thankfully, David and I loved the Lord individually before we decided to get married. David was a little more stubborn than me, but over time he fully surrendered to God. That helped us pray together, study together, worship together, and go to God about each other when we didn't know who else to go to.

The cord of your marriage is held together by the glue of God's grace. Your marriage has already proven to be a miracle, held together by God's love. The miracle of your marriage is that you should not have survived this far, but God has kept you together for a purpose.

When David and I met, we never knew the great things God had in store for us. We didn't know that thirty years later we would be traveling the world together, lifting up the name of Jesus, and bringing souls to Christ through so many different platforms. We didn't know that God would bless us the way he has. All we knew was that we loved each other. All we knew was that we loved God. If you love God and if you love each other, then you can make it through anything—the mountains, the valleys, the deserts, and the storms. With God all things are possible!

WILL YOU PRAY WITH US?

Father, thank you for the gift of faith. Thank you for the gift of love. When belief is combined with compassion, the consequence is blessing after blessing after blessing. Help me to continue to believe in my spouse. Help me to love through thick and thin. You have been the unbreakable cord that has kept us together. Without you, we can do nothing. In Jesus' name, amen.

DISCUSSION QUESTIONS

Questions for Wives

1. Do I pray for my husband daily?
2. Am I more inclined to try to get my husband to do what I want, or do I take our issues to God in prayer?
3. Does my husband dread seeing me when he first comes in the door, or is he excited?
4. Name an issue that requires a conversation versus an issue that requires consecration.
5. When have you been successful in praying for something to change and it did? What were you doing during that time while you were praying?
6. Before I confront my husband for something he isn't doing right, have I allowed God to work on me?

Questions for Husbands

1. Do I pray for my wife daily?
2. Do my children see me pray in the home?
3. Do we pray together as a family?
4. Am I covering my wife the way Christ covers the church?
5. In what way can I improve my devotional time with God?
6. Name an issue that requires a conversation versus an issue that requires consecration.

BONUS ACTIVITY: SETTING GOALS FOR YOUR MARRIAGE

We want to encourage you to go back and look at the areas in which you want to grow as a couple. In the chart below, list your thirty-day, one-year, and five-year goals for your marriage. Complete this activity with your spouse, and then plan a time when you will implement these goals.

Thirty-Day Goal	One-Year Goal	Five-Year Goal
Action plan to accomplish goal:	Action plan to accomplish goal:	Action plan to accomplish goal:

BONUS ACTIVITY: PRAYING TOGETHER

Think on ways to keep your marriage holy. Consider the ways that already work for you and your spouse. Write them down in the space provided in the following chart. As a couple, we have found power in working together, traveling together, praying together, raising kids together, worshiping together, and going to church and serving together. Identify the spiritual elements of your own marriage that help it to remain whole. Write down each of these in the following space.

Ways to Keep Our Marriage Holy:

Spiritual Elements That Keep Our Marriage Whole:

For the next seven days, pray with your spouse before leaving the house. If this is new to you, do not be concerned with the type of prayer you pray. Just pray from your heart. Speak to God with your spouse. If your spouse does not know the Lord, invite them to pray, but do not apply too much pressure. Just pray alone and directly pray specific prayers for your spouse to come around. Feel free to use the following space to jot down specific prayer requests to get started.

_____

_____

_____

_____

ACKNOWLEDGMENTS

First and foremost, we would like to thank our heavenly Father, who's the head of everything we do. It is your new mercies every day that have guided us on this beautiful thirty-year journey of marriage.

So many people have played a part in our thirty-year journey of life. We'd like to acknowledge those who have played a vital part along the way.

To all the *teams* that made this dream possible:

David Jr., Theland, Porcia, and Tia: We wouldn't be able to do what we do if it wasn't for you all.

TKO marketing team and Linda Klosterman Kirkpatrick: Thank you for your loyalty and continuous belief in us.

The Wright Group, Cherry Wright and the late Gerald Wright: Thank you for your guidance and for sticking in there with us when we didn't know what we were doing.

Roger Bobb and Bobbcat Films: Thanks for your continuous belief in us. We love you more than you will ever know. Let's make more shows.

Debra Shavers and A-plus travel, Cheryl Potts and Crystal Clear Music, Bonnie Berry LaMon and B2L Law: Thanks for dotting the i's and crossing the t's.

The Orchard distribution, and Damon Stewart and IGA: Thanks for getting us heard.

Keaston McKinney, De Lacy, The Glam Squad: Karla Langs, Riska Crowder, Toya Fennell, Fred Sanders, Krystal Gentry, DD Kelly, Maria Harper, Chassity Williams, Chantal Mann, and Melissa Amos.

To the *people* who have contributed:

Granny Charlie Mae Mann: Thank you for the early morning scriptures.

Nicole Jones: Without your introduction, there would be no *us* against the world.

Pastor Sherman Allen: Thanks for making this love official.

Theland Edwards: Thank you for the late night book notes and phone conversations. Thanks for helping us put everything together.

Shaun Saunders: Thanks for taking our story and bringing it to life.

Kirk Franklin: Your pen brought my voice to life. Love you, lil bro.

Tyler Perry: Sharing the stage with you helped us become better entertainers and all-around people.

Arthur Primus: Without you there is no *us* in this business.

Arthur Jones: Thanks for believing in us.

Jessie Hurst: Thanks for always being there for us, "cuz."

Helen Epps and Morning Star Prayer Center: Thanks for your many prayers.

Bill Carpenter, Angie Bones, and Phil Thornton: Thanks for all the advice and for being a listening ear.

Mama and Daddy Stone: Thanks for the guidance.

Uncle Robert and Dollie Sample, and my home church, Holy Tabernacle COGIC: Thanks for showing us what family looks like.

Aunt Ethel.

Cassandra Kelly: Thanks for the late-night songs.

Mark Sample, Nedra Nevels, and Jackie Birdow.

Our pastor and first lady, Darrell and LaTonja Blair: Thanks for thirty-plus years of brotherhood and friendship.

Our church family at New Breed Christian Center.

Myron Butler: Thank you for all the music.

JaVon Hill: Thanks for producing magic.

Bishop Vaughn McLaughlin: Thanks for the spot to lay our head.

Bishop Walker, Bishop Morton, Joni and Marcus Lamb, Pastor Joel Osteen, Pastor Freddy Haynes, Pastor Ricky Rush, Bishop T.D. Jakes, Pastor John Gray, Pastor Tony Evans, Terri Vaughn, Denise Boutte, Bishop Winans, Pastor Jenkins, Bishop Don Meares, Pastor Donnie McClurkin, and Priscilla Shirer.

The Johnsons, the Manns, the Cottrells, the Campbells, the Freemans, the Tribbetts, the Franklins, Wiley Williams and family, the Wrights, the Robinsons, the Hollins, and the Phillips.

ABOUT THE AUTHORS

DAVID AND TAMELA MANN are a dynamic husband-and-wife duo who have become household names across television and movie screens, on stage, and on radio. David is an ingeniously funny and extraordinarily talented actor/comedian, screenwriter, and director. His partner in life and business is Grammy Award–winning superstar Tamela Mann. Audiences have come to know and love David and Tamela via Kirk Franklin and the Family and Tyler Perry film and television productions. They are known for bringing good, old-fashioned family values, laughter, and music to whatever they do.

David's much-lauded comedic sensibility and accomplished performances have been recognized with an NAACP Image Award for Best Actor in a Comedy Series and the GMA Grady Nutt Humor Award. In addition to the Grammy win, Tamela, whose beautiful voice has inspired millions, has garnered NAACP Image, Billboard Music, and Soul Train Music Award wins, numerous Gospel Music Stellar and GMA Dove Awards, and RIAA Platinum and Gold *Billboard* number-one albums and singles. The music sensation set a historic personal and industry record as the first gospel lead artist in *Billboard* radio chart history to score three consecutive number ones from an album and for the most number ones in the history of *Billboard*'s Gospel Airplay chart.

Despite all the awards and accolades, David and Tamela agree their greatest accomplishment is their thirty-year marriage. In *Us Against the World: Our Secrets to Love, Marriage, and Family,* the couple shares their keys to maintaining a strong Christian marriage and family while juggling successful screen, stage, and music careers. David, Tamela, and their blended family of five adult kids and ten grandkids live in Dallas, Texas.

SHAUN SAUNDERS is the author of six books and has assisted more than three hundred authors by telling authentic, inspirational, and educational stories. The president of Finish Your Book Inc. and Godzchild Publications, Shaun is the professor of English literature at Caldwell College and Bloomfield College, and serves as the discipleship pastor at Change Church in Ewing, New Jersey. Whenever Shaun isn't writing, he is most likely spending time with his precocious six-year-old daughter, Zinai Esther.

Use the instructions below
to access your FREE audiobook
download of *Us Against the World*,
provided by Rakuten Kobo:

1. Visit www.UsAgainstTheWorldAudiobook.com.

2. Fill out and submit the form on the www.UsAgainstTheWorldAudiobook.com landing page.

3. Download your FREE audiobook using the download code and instructions that will be sent to your email.

4. Listen and enjoy!

All download codes expire on 11/13/2019.